Castles and Palaces

Germany

Schmid
Verlag

Germany

Dozens of popular books about castles offer readers a basically consistent, but nevertheless incorrect view of history. Our image of the Middle Ages, and hence of castles too, is to a large extent inaccurate, having more to do with the romantic imagination of the

which will accept it in confidence and good faith.

This book is different inasmuch as it takes this responsibility to its readers very seriously. It is not merely an uncritical collage of what other books have said before but rather is firmly based on the professional

more to offer than just forty castles and palaces. I have nevertheless attempted to include as interesting a variety of castles as possible, including several ruins. Not only do such ruined castles account for one third of the total, but they also tend to attract us and inspire us much

Castles and Palaces

18th and 19th centuries than with reality. Those who write books about castles and palaces, however, are bound not only by the dictates of good journalism but also by the need to educate their readers. Such authors must be aware that they are making information accessible to a wide readership

work being done on countless castles and palaces. Much of the information provided here is indeed the result of research which has either not been published at all or only in academic journals.

Yet far from being dry and scholarly, this book instead seeks to be both readable and entertaining. It aims to educate by correcting old assumptions and replacing them, where necessary, with what we now know to be the truth.

It goes without saying that the castles and palaces in this book were selected according to extremely subjective criteria. Germany has far

more than do their intact counterparts. For castle researchers too, ruins are especially interesting. They provide us with a snapshot of a particular period, unencumbered by destructive conversion and extension work, their bare walls unsullied by modern rendering.

Dr. Joachim Zeune

The numbers entered in the map refer to the page on which the particular castle or palace is described.

Hamburg

30

Weser

Elbe

Havel

Ems

Havel

Berlin

26

28

Hannover

32

Oder

Weser

Leine

40

Spree

20

Elbe

44

Saale

Leipzig

46

Dortmund

34

18

Dresden

36

106

12

14

10

Köln

Rhein

102

22

8

38

60

64

104

50

56

Frankfurt

Main

48

66

100

54

68

76

Nürnberg

80

74

82

Stuttgart

84

Neckar

70

Donau

Isar

88

94

98

München

92

96

Inn

Chiemsee

Bodensee

The full names and addresses of the castles and palaces shown on this map are listed at the end of the book.

Festung Königstein -
where Germany's largest wine cask once stood

View from the west: Huge bastions and three drawbridges protected the outer gate (left) from which a ramp cut into the cliff led up onto the plateau. The fortifications on top of the plateau contain the Georgenburg (left, built in 1619), the Magdalenenburg (centre rear, built 1622/23), the Old Barracks (centre, built 1589), the Old Armory (right, built in 1594), the Friedrichsburg (left rear, built in 1589 and converted in 1731), the Garrison Church (centre rear, with remains of the 13th century chapel) as well as several barracks and extensive casemates.

Towering above the banks of the river Elbe not far from Dresden, there is a huge plateau whose sheer cliffs imperceptibly give way to a battlemented parapet surrounding an area of 9.5 hectares. As this natural bulwark, upgraded by the addition of a man-made fortress, is located at a strategically advantageous point for both river and road traffic, it has had a vital role to play from the military point of view throughout the centuries.

The first documentary evidence of the castle dates back to 1241, when the Bohemian King Wenceslas I mentioned it in a deed as the "lapide regis", or "King's Rock", although archaeological excavations indicate that it was already in existence even in the 12th century. The fortifications added between the 16th and 20th centuries largely removed the medieval castle, which attracted the little town which still exists at the foot of the pla-

was not among them, as he had long since wriggled out of the trap...

In the years which followed, numerous Saxon margraves, dukes and electors added buildings to Festung Königstein and even during the German Reich, the fortress was modernized before being abandoned for good as a defensive installation in 1913.

The Elector Friedrich August I, also known as August the Strong and as notorious for his profligacy as for his bragging, even went so far as to draw up plans for the conversion of the monstrous grey Königstein into a splendid Baroque palace. In 1722, however, these plans had to be sacrificed to his determination to win the so-called "Cask War" at all costs. The point of this highly publicized competition between the Elector of the

Since 1955, Königstein has housed a museum containing an interesting collection of weapons, among other things. It is above all the magnificent views, however, and spectacular, cliff-top architecture which attract some half a million visitors to the fortress year in year out.

teau as early as 1379. The Königstein's legendary unassailability was first put to the test in 1403. This was when Margrave Wilhelm I of Meissen attacked the castle in an attempt to evict the seditious Captain Jeschke von Dohna, who had entrenched himself there. The precipitous cliffs, however, proved an insuperable bulwark, given that this was before the days of heavy artillery. Armed only with cross-bows, long bows, muskets, mortars and scaling ladders, the gigantic natural fortress could not be conquered. This left only the most tedious and most expensive of all the methods available: The fortress would have to be encircled and besieged until its starving occupants surrendered of their own accord. Yet it was only after four years of extreme hardship that those defending the castle, demoralized by hunger, finally surrendered. Jeschke von Dohna, however,

Palatinate and the Elector of Saxony was to establish which of them should have the dubious honour of building the larger wine cask. In 1725, August the Strong finally triumphed when he built a gigantic wine cask with a capacity of 238,000 litres in one of the Königstein's cellars (cf. Heidelberg!).

This inhospitable, cliff-top fortress, which was visited by the Russian Tsar Peter I in 1698 and 1706 and by Napoleon in 1813 to inspect ist famous fortifications, has repeatedly served as a prison throughout its history.

Stolpen -
prison for an unwanted mistress

View of the main castle. The Seiger Tower (begun 1455, enlarged 1560) is visible in the foreground, while the Johannis or Cosel Tower, built in 1509, can be seen to the right. In 1562, a clock was added to the Seiger Tower, although the clock face is now located in the inner ward.

The many-towered silhouette of Burg Stolpen can be seen high up on its curious basalt pedestal for miles around. This geological phenomenon and the remarkable monument it supports, are now popular tourist attractions, not least on account of the highly varied programme of "events" on offer as well as the spacious museum. Whether it is legitimate to present such popular but unrealistic attractions as the torture chamber, however, a "feature" which castles never had prior to the 16th century - and then only in exceptional cases, is open to question. Most torture chambers were installed in the 19th and 20th centuries to make castles more gruesome and hence more exciting for tourists.

Also open to question is whether the Germans really did build a castle made of "geschrothetem Holze", or "scrap wood" to defend themselves against the Bohemians in the year 1121. What is known is that in the 13th century, the Bishopric of Meissen began developing its newly acquired domain of Stolpen by building a castle. It was not until the year 1559, however, that the Elector August I acquired this strategically important office by shrewdly exchanging it for another and so was able to start work on the conversion of the Burg Stolpen into a fortified Renaissance castle. What was decisive was the refashioning of the first inner ward which began in 1675. The impressive fortress to which this gave rise, however, lasted less than a century, certain parts of it having to be demolished as early as 1773.

In 1813, Napoleon had this strategically important castle repaired, but destroyed it again shortly afterwards as part of the scorched earth policy practised during the retreat from Russia. This was not the first time the castle had been destroyed. After all, just about all the major wars to have taken place since the Hussite raids (around 1429) had inflicted visible damage.

The castle became famous as the "safekeeping" of the Countess of Cosel, an unusually pretty, intelligent and self-confident woman. The Elector August the Strong was so overwhelmed by this young beauty that in 1705, head over heels in love, he was persuaded to give her a written promise of marriage. When the Countess began interfering in his lifestyle, however, and when he found Magdalene von Dönhoff to be an equally appealing but far less demanding mistress, the Elector August asked to be released from the betrothal. The proud Countess, however, insisted that the contract be upheld, with the result that the Elector August had no choice but to remove her from the public eye and imprison her at Burg Stolpen. Her involuntary sojourn at the castle, whose "Cosel Tower" is a reminder of her presence there, did not end until her death in 1765.

Almost nothing is left of the original castle, built in the High Middle Ages. The towers originate from the years shortly after 1450 and were built specifically for the use of fire-arms. Especially remarkable are the four consecutive inner wards and the "waterworks", built in 1561-63, which pumped water up to the castle from a spring 700 metres away and 100 metres further down the valley.

The Countess Cosel's kitchen on the first floor of the Johannis or Cosel Tower. Only the interior architecture is really old. The fur-

nishings are a recent addition, the idea being to illustrate how the Countess Cosel must have lived. Anna von Cosel died in 1765 at the age of 84, after 49 years of imprisonment at Burg Stolpen.

Gnandstein -
jewel of a castle

To describe Gnandstein as pretty or even picturesque would be absurd: This monstrous grey edifice situated on a low spur of the Erz Mountains is scarcely an inviting sight. And yet the castle is well worth a visit, if only because of what it tells us about the history of architecture. Furthermore, it now houses an interesting museum, consisting of several rooms in Baroque or late-Gothic style, a wonderful chapel, a great hall restored in Romanesque style, a collection of antique furniture and works of art and an interesting exhibition on castles.

Like nearly all castles, it took centuries of building, rebuilding and expansion before Gnandstein acquired the imposing shape it has today. It was founded in 1200 by the Margraves of Meissen, who wanted a small, curtained castle from which to expand and consolidate their lordship. Some fifty years later, the castle was upgraded in line with the latest developments in defensive architecture and the front wall enlarged to such an

extent that it soon came to resemble a shield held up in front of the rest of the castle. An even higher round tower was built immediately behind this "shield wall", thus enhancing not only the castle's defences but also the imposing and intimidating impression left by the front facade. On the south side, on the other hand, a small but attractive great hall was built, both splendid enough for representative purposes and comfortable enough to be habitable.

Around 1400, Gnandstein passed to the Lords of Einsiedel and remained in their hands until it was expropriated in 1945. This family for a long time ranked among the most important and most affluent of Saxony's nobility, it having been above all Heinrich of Einsiedel, Lord of Gnandstein between 1461 and 1507, who greatly increased the family's possessions. The esteem he enjoyed as privy councillor to the Electors of Saxony enabled him to acquire a stake in several silver mines and so to

Gnandstein is now one of the most important castles in Saxony. Its huge, gloomy walls tower above the surrounding countryside. The front of the castle - that facing the enemy - is protected by a tower positioned immediately behind a huge shield wall, both of which structures date back to the mid-13th century. The fortress became a residential castle under Heinrich von Einsiedel from 1461 onwards. The medieval castle with its Romanesque great hall, keep, curtain wall and shield wall, have retained their impressive appearance. The same is true of the interior furnishings added in the centuries to follow. Today, the castle houses an interesting museum of the Free State of Saxony.

How much and how often was determined by law. As both sides were dependent on the other and so had a vested interest in the other's well-being, they lived more-or-less peacefully in a purposeful and healthy symbiosis right up until the 14th century. It was then that the growing prosperity of the cities and ascendancy of the princes as well as new economic structures and agricultural crises led to the widespread impoverishment of the nobility and hence to the emergence of the notorious robber knights. More and more feudal lords believed themselves compelled to exploit their villeins as ruthlessly as possible. The peasants, however, still reeling from the effects of the plague and other natural catastrophes and now faced with a genuinely existential crisis, took courage from the ideas of the Reformation and finally rose up in 1525 in a poorly organized and doomed revolt against their masters. Despite the support they received

The late-Gothic chapel, built in 1501-03 and carefully restored in 1968, is among the most imposing buildings at Burg Gnandstein. Heinrich of Einsiedel, the man who commissioned it, had a side altar built for each of this three wives. The impressive Mary's Altar was carved by Peter Breuer while the paintings are the work of an unknown master.

amass a huge private fortune. It was under him that Gnandstein was transformed into a respectable castle dwelling.

His successor, Heinrich Hildebrand (1497-1557), has gone down in history as a truly remarkable personality, whose humanist education and friendship with Martin Luther caused him to adopt an unusually liberal attitude towards the villeins on his demesne. The labour and taxes exacted so unscrupulously and with such arrogant presumption by other lords at that time proved such a burden on Heinrich's conscience that shortly before his death in 1557, he bequeathed a number of important endowments to the various villages in his lordship.

The peasants' revolt had swept over central and southern Germany and been brutally suppressed just thirty-two years previously. Since time immemorial, the villeins had been bound to render their lords not only produce (and later even monetary dues as well), but also their labour and the use of their oxen.

from certain knights, among them the famous Götz von Berlichingen or Florian Geyer, the peasants were inexperienced in the arts of war. Poorly armed and fighting mainly in uncoordinated groups, they never constituted a serious threat to the armies of the nobility. Flails and pitchforks are no match for halberds and arquebus - it was bound to end badly. Not only did the peasants gain nothing, but they even had to pay heavily for the damage they had caused.

It should also be remembered, however, that in the golden age of chivalry, meaning from the 11th to 13th centuries, the situation had been very different. At that time, robber knights and exploited peasants were the exception rather than the rule. Furthermore, as those who built castles were bound by law to reward the services rendered by their villeins, the building of a castle was generally a risky undertaking with costs running into the order of millions.

Zwinger in Dresden –
a very special festival ground

Elector August the Strong went down in history as an ostentatious, vainglorious ruler and hence a typical example of an absolutist prince. He is also the monarch most closely associated with Dresden's outstanding examples of Baroque architecture. After being crowned King of Poland in 1697, he found Dresden's old-fashioned Stadtschloss to be inadequate to his new social requirements and political ambitions.

To provide his court with an appropriately pompous and contemporary setting, August had several castles and palaces built in and around Dresden, all of which are now known collectively as "Augustan Baroque" and are considered among the finest and most important examples of Baroque architecture in Germany.

Dresden's much-admired Zwinger Palace was also a product - indeed the culmination - of August's mania for building. Its special function differentiated it, at least in architectural terms, from other Baroque buildings: It was to serve not just as a residence but as a festival ground too, and therefore constituted a sophisticated combination of festive and garden architecture - a kind of outdoor festival hall. It was here that pleasure-loving Baroque courtiers pursued their various pastimes, here that chivalric tournaments were held and theatre productions staged - to say nothing of the equestrian ballets so highly prized by the King himself.

The name "Zwinger" is attributable to the palace's location outside Dresden's fortifications. In military jargon, the word "Zwinger" means the space between two walls of enceinte. Today, only the old pond and moat are left to remind us of the huge bastions, walls and ditches which once belonged to Dresden's now vanished fortifications.

The Baroque stone buildings of the so-called Zwinger Palace actually had a direct predecessor in the form of a wooden amphitheatre erected in 1709 for a visit of the Danish King Friedrich IV. It was in this Colosseum that the royal guest was treated to the spectacular "Ladies' Carousel" - a Roman-style chariot race in which contemporary VIPs raced chariots carrying distinguished ladies. King Friedrich himself, for example, raced a chariot containing the Elector's mistress, Anna Constanze, Countess Cosel, assisted by no lesser person than the Elector himself, who in this case acted only as the outrider.

The lovers were so happy and carefree back then - who could have guessed the sad fate awaiting this young but power-hungry mistress in the years to come (cf. Stolpen!)

View from the east over the Baroque festival ground to the famous Wall Pavilion (background). This is flanked by the Pavilion of Mathematics and Physics (left) and the French Pavilion (right), which now houses a café. Dresden's Zwinger Palace was built in 1711-1728 by order of Elector August the Strong and is considered an absolute tour de force of Baroque architecture.

The small dome of the Crown Gate was decorated to resemble a crown. This in turn supports a smaller crown, surrounding by four eagles to symbolize the Polish monarchy, conferred upon Elector August the Strong in 1697.

These magnificent festivities closed with a splendid fireworks display, which spectators were invited to admire from the vantage point of barges on the river Elbe.

August the Strong had this temporary wooden building replaced by a new palace, made of stone, the construction of which was incumbent upon the state's own architect, Matthäus Daniel Pöppelmann. August started by sending Pöppelmann to Vienna and Rome to inspect the most recent palaces and gardens there and familiarize himself with the latest architectural trends. Dresden's court sculptor, Permoser, who had spent 14 years gathering experience in naturalistic sculpture in Venice, Rome and Florence, also had an important role to play in the building of the Zwinger.

Work on the Zwinger began in 1711 and ended seventeen years later. Originally, it was to have been just part of a much larger and more ambitious building project, although this was never in fact executed.

The art gallery built by Gottfried Semper in 1847-54 contains a collection of famous old masters, including the

"Sistine Madonna" by Raphael (1483-1520), one of the most famous painters of the Italian Renaissance.

Pöppelmann created a rectangular festival ground, framed by symmetrically arranged, single-storey galleries and two-storey pavilions. The main entrance is on the south side, where visitors enter through the two-storey Crown Gate, the dome of which was decorated to resemble a huge crown. On top of this dome, a second, smaller crown was added, surrounded by four eagles - the symbol of the Polish monarchy.

The Pavilion of Mathematics and Physics, the Wall Pavilion, French Pavilion and grotto-like Nymphs' Bath are all on the west side. The latter of these consisted of a small cascade decorated with dolphins, Tritons, naiades and nymphs derived from Greek mythology.

The east side is arranged identically with a Pavilion of Zoology, Glockenspiel Pavilion and German Pavilion. The second of these owes its name to the glockenspiel suspended inside it, which is made up of 40 bells made of Meissen porcelain.

The north side of the palace was originally left open to permit superb views of the nearby river Elbe. The famous architect, Gottfried Semper, however, blocked this view by adding an art gallery, which now houses a collection of old masters and a historical museum.

It is the Wall Pavilion on the west wide which, thanks to its splendid architecture and ornate design, its vibrant facades and roofs radiating an almost Rococco-style joviality, forms the eye-catching, architectural highlight of the palace. After passing through the open ground floor, visitors will find ingenious staircases leading to both the neighbouring pavilions and the fortifications.

Permoser's sculptures and his mingling of political symbols (coats-of-arms) with figures from ancient mythology, served primarily to glorify his absolutist patron. Like many great princes of the age of absolutism, August the Strong liked to see himself personified as the powerful demigod, Hercules (cf. Wilhelmshöhe). Others again preferred to have themselves depicted as Apollo, god of the muses.

In 1719, the marriage of the young crown prince Friedrich August to the Archduchess Maria Josepha, daughter of Kaiser Joseph I, was celebrated on the grounds of the partially finished Zwinger.

Notwithstanding such magnificent festivities, the Zwinger went into decline shortly after August's death in 1733. Its bombardment during the Seven Years' War (1756-1763) naturally proved far more catastrophic, as did above all the appalling destruction wrought by the bombing of Dresden in February 1945, when much of the Zwinger was severely damaged.

The meticulous and laborious process of reconstruction was completed in 1964, although the palace now has its own site hut which takes care of the preservation of this world-famous architectural and cultural monument.

Querfurt - the towered castle

The mighty and above all many-towered Burg Querfurt ranks among those few castles which stand a chance of according with our misconception of what constitutes a "genuine" medieval castle. The only fly in the ointment is the fact that, despite its position on top of a shell-limestone promontery, it is scarcely higher than the town surrounding it and therefore looks more like a town with lots of towers than a real castle.

The vastness of this castle is a result of its origins as an early-medieval defensive enclosure. Then, in the last decades prior to the end of the first millenium, a family of free nobles settled inside the fortress, named themselves after their castle and retained it right up to the year 1496. During this period, the family grew and acquired ever more power and influence, as is apparent from the castle architecture.

Comprehensive research, including archaeological digs, has turned up evidence of a stone castle dating from the 10th and 11th centuries, consisting of a curtain wall, several residential buildings, a gatehouse and a small church. Over the centuries, this "original castle" was steadily enlarged, primarily by the addition of towers. These include the main tower, a bulging

The silhouette of Burg Querfurt is easily identifiable on account of its. The oldest of these is the so-called "Dicke Heinrich", or "Fat Henry", dating from the second half of the 12th century (far left). To the right, there is the so-called "Marterturm", or "Tower of Agony", and in the background, the bulbous cupola of the "Paris Tower" is also just visible. The bastion in the foreground was built in the last quarter of the 15th century, when the castle was enlarged to make it suitable for artillery.

The west gate with its huge embrasures for light artillery, built in the second half of the 15th century, is particularly well fortified. The outside wall was originally very ornate.

round tower known as "Dicke Heinrich", or "Fat Henry", which has walls over four metres thick and contains neither windows nor chimneys, lavatories, stairs or a vault - and hence was uninhabitable. German castle research has traditionally described such towers as "keeps", their purpose being purely defensive. Not only were such keeps intended to make an active contribution to the defence of the castle, but they could also serve as the refuge of last resort in the event of imminent danger.

This theory, however, is refuted by the fact that few keeps contain defensive elements such as embrasures, machicolations or battlemented "combat platforms". Not only that, many of them are actually quite small. Furthermore, they are always characterized by excellent stone-masonry - which would be odd, if they were intended merely as fortifications.

The fact is, that ever since the famous Tower of Babel, towers have been regarded as a symbol of pure power. Even today, the big banks and multinationals still vie to see who can build the highest skyscraper as concrete proof of both market hegemony and wealth. The castle tower, however, was more than just a symbol. It also served as a lookout and safe as well as a dungeon in which to keep prisoners. It provided protection without, however, being able to defend itself to any great extent, its primary function therefore being to impress and intimidate.

Burg Querfurt was not properly fortified until around 1460, when its fortifications were upgraded by the addition of bastions and heavily fortified gates. Today, the castle is restored and operational and contains a museum.

Bernburg -
where Till Eulenspiegel blew his own trumpet

The reunification of Germany has made countless important cultural monuments in what used to be East Germany once again accessible to all. What had once been a cohesive cultural landscape was split apart pointlessly and by force by the Berlin Wall, thus creating two German states instead of one.

Among the most outstanding cultural monuments in the German state of Saxony-Anhalt is the Renaissance Bernburg, built on a high, sandstone outcrop above the banks of the river Saale.

The castle is made up of a dense clutch of whitewashed buildings with such typical Renaissance features as gables, oriels and regular rows of windows, repeatedly interrupted by much older, beige-coloured stonework. It is clear that here at the Bernburg, old and new were mingled together to create a conglomerate - a combination of styles which is most clearly apparent in the enormous keep. Despite its dainty gabled roof, this huge

The silhouette of the castle is predominated by the whitewashed Renaissance buildings and much older stonework. A castle on this site mentioned in documents dated 961 was burned down by the Saxons and then rebuilt in 1138. From 1245 onwards, however, the Bernburg served as the primary residence of the Bernburg line of the princes of Anhalt and later, until 1765, of the princes of Anhalt-Bernburg. Today, the revitalized castle contains a museum of local history devoted primarily to local mills as well as an important collection of minerals. The concerts held here are also extremely popular.

round tower cannot disguise the even greater age of its massive walls. It is just too big, too grand and much too grave in comparison with the ornate buildings surrounding it. Indeed, the keep is the best preserved part of the castle which used to stand on this site, a castle which between 1538/39 and 1570 was transformed into the impressive Renaissance palace visible today.

The Thirty Years' War from 1618 to 1648 was a terrible time for Europe, as also for the Bernburg, which was stormed and damaged no fewer than three times in 1636 and 1641. Having been triggered by confessional differences, the war actually consisted of a whole series of smaller wars. Both Protestant and Catholic alliances were created and as each was able to call in the support of powerful allies, it did not take long before various European powers were engaged in battles on German soil which had less to do with Germany than with the political interests of the combatants. On the one side there was the Catholic League and the kaiser, supported by the Spanish Habsburgs and on the other, the Protestant Union, supported initially by Denmark, the Netherlands and England and later by Sweden and ultimately even France. The Catholic generals Tilly and Wallenstein acquired almost legendary fame for their feats during this period.

By the time the so-called Peace of Westphalia put an end to the war in 1648, it was not only the house of Habsburg which had been defeated, but also - and above all - the German economy. Nearly half the population had been wiped out and the countryside laid waste. Gangs of marauding, "unemployed" mercenaries continued to plunder the land for years to come. France and Sweden, however, profited both economically and politically from the demise of the German empire.

Prince Christian I of Anhalt-Bernburg (1568/1603-1630), had an important role to play in the Thirty Years' War. As Governor of the Upper Palatinate, it was he who created the Protestant Union and in 1620 fought - and lost - the first battle of the war at Weissen Berg near Prague.

Bernburg, however, has also been the scene of many amusing and peaceful incidents as well. In the 22nd History of Till Eulenspiegel, for example, we are told how the famous prankster was employed as town trumpeter by Prince Bernhard of Anhalt. Compared to the sumptuous banquets and exquisite wines served to the prince himself, however, both the pay and the meagre diet offered to such lowly servants as Till left a lot to be desired.

One day, Till Eulenspiegel was up in his tower when he once again got a whiff of the delectable dishes being prepared for the prince in the castle kitchens. Deciding on impulse that this was too much to bear, he grabbed his horn and sounded the alarm. Once the distinguished gentlemen had fled their table, Till took their place and tucked into the opulent repast. With no-one to disturb him, he was finally able to eat his fill - before departing the castle never to be seen again. Since then, the people of Bernburg have called the keep the "Eulenspiegel Tower".

The oldest book version of Till Eulenspiegel's Merry Pranks dates from around 1530, although the story itself can be traced back to the 13th or 14th century. The 96 satirical tales poking fun at late medieval society are the work of an unknown author from the Braunschweig region and were extremely popular right from the start.

The locals refer to Bernburg's massive keep as the "Eulenspiegel Tower", because it was here that the famous prankster is alleged to have served as town trumpeter. It was in this capacity that he once sounded the alarm in order to entice his lord and master away from the dinner table, so that he himself could finish the delectable dishes on the menu that day. The huge, grey walls of the tower date back to around 1200 and are in stark contrast to the delicate, ornamental style of the Renaissance pediments built between 1538/39 and 1570.

Altenburg -
scene of the abduction of the Saxon princes

The Altenburg in Thuringia has a history going back over a thousand years. The porphyritic precipice on which it now stands, towering above the town of the same name, was used for fortifications as long ago as the Early Middle Ages, when the Slavic Sorbs built a huge bulwark there. The German kings recognized its strategic importance in the 10th century, when they erected a fortress here from which to govern the surrounding demesne. Over the years, this fortress was elevated to the status of a "Kaiserpfalz", or imperial palace. King Lothar III, for example, held court here in 1132.

The Altenburg was to retain its lofty position within the empire under successive German kings and kaisers thereafter. Kaiser Friedrich I, for example, whose red beard earned him the name "Barbarossa", resided here no fewer than six times between the years 1165 and 1188.

It was from this castle that missionaries were dispatched to convert the heathen Slavs using both peaceful and forceful means. In 1327, this christianization resulted in the banning of the Slavic language, although not even this was enough to prevent the intermingling of what were fundamentally different cultures.

In those days, the county of Thuringia and hence the Altenburg were held by the Wettin Margraves of Meissen. The history of the castle up to the year 1603, when it became the centre of an independent principality and ultimately a duchy, was shaped largely by a number of highly complicated divisions of land and estates.

The Altenburg became famous beyond the borders of Thuringia as the scene of the abduction of the Saxon princes - a spectacular kidnapping in the late Middle Ages which has been the subject of over 40 plays.

The chief protagonist was Kunz of Kauffungen, a belligerent rake of a knight with a keen eye to his own advantage. In 1446, he threw in his lot with the Elector of Saxony, Friedrich the Gentle, in a war against the latter's brother - naturally on the assumption that this would help further his political career as well as lining his pockets. Things turned out quite differently, however. Kunz had the great misfortune to be taken prisoner by the enemy and had to ransom himself to the tune of 4,000 gold gulden.

The imposing Schloss Altenburg is a conglomerate of buildings dating from various periods. The oldest of them, including a huge round tower known locally as the "bottle", date back to the High Middle Ages. The south wing was erected on the south-western corner of the fortress in the 16th and early 17th centuries. The late Gothic church adjoining this wing boasts a splendid Baroque organ and a magnificent vaulted ceiling.

As his only interest in this particular war had been to support his Elector, he understandably believed himself entitled to demand the reimbursement of this huge ransom from Friedrich. The Elector, however, for his part, did not see any reason to comply with this demand and, taking the view that it was Kunz's own fault he had been captured in the first place, flatly refused to pay up. The situation was further exacerbated when the knight's own properties were badly damaged in the course of the same war and some merchants he had imprisoned in his own Schloss Stein were set free before he had had time to extort a ransom. Kunz tried to make the Elector liable for this incident too, at which point Friedrich lost all trace of the gentleness for which he was renowned and handed the matter over to a

A view into the Johann Sebastian Bach Hall, built inside the south wing of the residence in the early 17th century. After a fire in 1905, the hall was redesigned by a famous masterbuilder in neo-Renaissance style. It is now used for concerts and recitals, much to the delight of Altenburg's music lovers.

court of arbitration which found against the now furious knight.

This was the last straw for Kunz. Desperate for revenge, he joined forces with two other malcontents, with whom he conspired to abduct the Elector's two young sons in order to be able to extort a hefty ransom for their release. Kunz had to bribe a kitchen boy to spy for him and provide him with the information he needed for his plot. This was how he found out that on July 7, 1455, the Elector was to travel to Leipzig, that the guards regularly got drunk on beer and that the gatekeeper was poorly. Kunz and his fellow conspirators immediately took steps to "legalize" their crime by dispatching a challenge to the Elector and that same night secretly entered the castle. They managed to abduct the princes without difficulty and were able to escape almost unnoticed. Once outside the castle, the kidnappers separated into two groups, each of which set off in the direction of nearby Bohemia. It did not take long before the alarm bells were ringing, however, and before messengers and search troops were in action throughout the country.

Kunz met his fate at the Grünhain Monastery where he was recognized and promptly arrested. The other group did not fare much better, being forced to give themselves up after unsuccessfully seeking refuge in a cave.

Although the two princes were able to return to Schloss Altenburg unharmed, Kunz was sentenced to death for breaching the public peace and was beheaded in the market square in Freiburg on July 14. The prosecution justified this harsh sentence on the grounds that the Elector had not received the challenge until the day after the kidnapping. This meant that not only had the abduction been unlawful, but the Elector had not been given sufficient time to prepare himself in a manner befitting his station.

The treacherous kitchen boy, however, is alleged to have been immured alive in the walls of the castle. This, of course, is just a legend, but one that fits in well with our image of the Middle Ages as a gloomy and barbaric era.

What are still found in castles from time to time are the bones of dogs buried inside the walls or in the cellars. It was customary for such unfortunate curs to be killed and built into the castle in the belief that such a sacrifice would protect the edifice from calamity and hardship. When the gate of Schloss Burgk collapsed in 1739, for example, a mummified dog was found in the middle of the wall. The dog had obviously been buried inside a small cavity when the building was enlarged in 1403 and had thus been doomed to keep watch over the castle for all eternity. Sacrificial customs such as these have a long tradition going back to pagan times.

Also of pagan origin are the stone masks and grotesque heads to be found on castle gates and towers throughout the centuries, the purpose of which was to keep evil spirits and other unwelcome visitors at bay.

No-one knows whether the walls of Schloss Altenburg contain such a sacrifice. At any rate, both the fortress and the castle which followed it were blessed by good fortune - apart from the occasional fire here and there - meaning that eight centuries' of architecture complete with some costly interiors have been preserved right down to this day. The castle now houses an interesting museum of playing cards as well as a exhibition of items from the ducal armory and a collection of antiques. The town of Altenburg, by the way, has always had a special interest in playing cards. Not only was it here that the game of skat was invented back in 1810, but in 1832, a world famous playing card factory opened in this very same town.

The castle church provides a venue for annual organ concerts during the summer months, the popularity of which is attributable not least to the church's wonderful Baroque organ. No lesser person than Johann Sebastian Bach himself was full of praise for this instrument with its 2000 pipes, built in 1739 by Heinrich Gottfried Trost. As Organist to the Court, his pupil, Johann Ludwig Krebs, continued to play on it right up to his death in 1780. The organ, which has since been superbly well restored and can now once again be played on all its registers, is considered one of the most beautiful-sounding Baroque organs in Germany.

This painting depicts an event at Schloss Altenburg dating back to the year 1180, namely the investiture of Otto of Wittelsbach with the Duchy of Bavaria by the Kaiser Friedrich I, also known as "Barbarossa" on account of his red beard. This marked the founding of what was to become the ducal and later royal house of Wittelsbach. "Barbarossa" paid numerous visits to the Altenburg and often conducted his affairs of state from apartments within the castle.

Schloss Charlottenburg -
the Queen's summer residence

The splendid dome crowning the central tract can be seen here behind the equestrian statue of the Elector Friedrich Wilhelm the Great. The dome was added in 1702 by the architect, Eosander von Göthe, as a pointer to the royal status of the man who commissioned it. It is crowned by a reproduction of the Goddess of Fortune, the original statue having been destroyed in 1943. The equestrian statue, sculpted by Andreas Schlüter in 1697 and cast in a single mould by Johann Jakobi around 1700, was originally positioned in front of the Berlin Stadtschloss, demolished in 1955.

For today's visitors, it is hard to imagine that this palace, now situated in the middle of a big city, was once surrounded by idyllic countryside and that it was the nearby village of Lietzow which gave it its original name of Lietzenburg.

The Elector Friedrich II of Brandenburg built this palace - then much smaller than it is now - in 1695-99 as a summer residence for his second wife, Sophie Charlotte. At that time, the building consisted of no more than what is now the central tract and was of course surrounded by the palace gardens.

Two years after the palace was completed, the Elector Friedrich was crowned the first King of Prussia. This brought about a change not only of social status but also of architectural style, which henceforth would have to meet the representative requirements typical of royalty. In 1702, therefore, he began enlarging the once modest Lietzenburg and turned it into a splendid royal castle, soon bustling with the social and courtly activities of Sophie Charlotte. Her greatest passions were for music and philosophy, theatre and opera as well as extravagent balls and banquets. She was a close friend of Gottfried Wilhelm Leibniz, the philosopher and founder of the Berlin Academy of Sciences, who, after her premature death in 1705, declared that he had never before seen such a wise and affable princess as she. In remembrance of his culturally sophisticated and accomplished wife, King Friedrich I renamed the Lietzenburg Charlottenburg. Four years later, he received a visit from King Friedrich IV of Denmark and Friedrich August II of Poland at Schloss Charlottenburg.

The transformation of what had been a summer residence into a splendid royal palace was the work of the architect, Johann Friedrich Eosander von Göthe, a native of Sweden but educated in Paris. He extended the old building by adding an extra wing on each side to create a contemporary, three-winged palace with an especially long facade facing the garden in the manner of the famous Palace of Versailles. It was also Eosander von Göthe who was responsible for the addition of the 48-metre-high dome, which greatly enhanced the impact of the castle when viewed from afar, especially as it was situated at the apex of a star-shaped network of avenues. Behind the palace, there is a park extending as far as the River Spree, which also feeds the numerous fountains and canals.

Inside the palace, Friedrich I commissioned not only richly decorated function rooms and residential quarters but also a highly ornamental chapel and magnificent porcelain cabinet. There were collections of this kind in nearly all Berlin's castles at this time, but only in Charlottenburg was such a cabinet preserved.

The son of Friedrich and Sophie Charlotte, King Friedrich Wilhelm I, showed no interest whatsoever in his parents' castle and left it to go to wrack and ruin. His successor, on the other hand, King Friedrich II, also known as Frederick the Great, moved into the palace he loved so much on May 31, 1740, that being the very first day of his reign, with the intention of enlarging it still further and of spending most of his life there. It was under him that the remarkable New Wing with its Golden Gallery and White Room were built. The more this introverted King withdrew from society, however, the more he sought refuge in his lonely little Schloss Sanssouci in Potsdam, which was eventually to become his permanent home. The much larger Charlottenburg thus came to be used only for large, official, family celebrations.

At the end of the 18th century, King Friedrich Wilhelm II decided to ameliorate the palace's rigorous symmetry. The fact that in the garden in particular, natural diversity had been sacrificed to the demand for rigid order, was completely at odds with his desire to experience nature first hand. This was very much in keeping with the spirit of the age. Whereas the 17th and 18th centuries had come to perceive mathematics, and with it geometry and symmetry, as the sole basis of all things and, after so many wars, had craved stability and order more than anything else, the late 18th century marked the beginning of a movement in the other direction, which deliberately turned its back on rationality and predictable structures. In Charlottenburg, this led to the garden being redesigned with "natural", meandering paths, a romantic viewing tower and two, ornate angling huts.

The Mausoleum built by Friedrich Schinkel contains the tombs of Queen Luise and King Friedrich Wilhelm III as well as the remains of Kaiser Wilhelm I

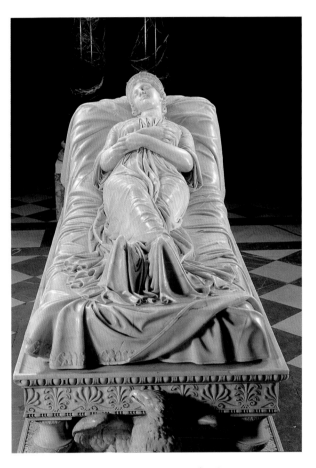

and his wife, the Kaiserin Augusta. The splendid sarcophagus of Queen Luise, who died in 1810, was the work of the sculptor, Christian Daniel Rauch.

Heavy bombing on November 23, 1943 destroyed within a matter of minutes everything it had taken generations of Prussian Kings to create or transform. The years that followed were devoted to laborious and expensive reconstruction and restoration work, most of which has now been completed. Several rooms, however, have been lost for good as there are no photographs remaining to remind us of how they once looked.

Sanssouci –
the carefree castle

The foundation stone for this pleasure castle, which was to serve King Friedrich II as a summer residence from 1747 onwards, was laid on April 1, 1745. The low, ground-floor castle is situated at the top of a terraced vineyard.

The central tract contains the great Marble Room, which was not finished until 1748. Its dome was modelled on the Roman Pantheon. The walls are lined with Corinthian double columns and the floor is made of coloured marble.

In the mid-18th century, just as the age of absolutism was drawing to a close, when kaisers, kings and princes still ruled the world like demigods and their craving for splendour, ostentation and indulgence was subject to only the most modest restrictions, their extravagant lifestyle at last began to take a toll - rather an odd one, admittedly, but better than nothing! Exhausted by an endless chain of social events, fed up with the hustle and bustle of court life and its parasitic courtiers, bored stiff by the rigour and inflexibility of court etiquette, the tedium and chicanery of bureaucratic obligations and the laborious business of governance, more and more rulers began to flee their huge palaces, preferring instead their smaller and more intimate rural seats.

As retreats, these rural castles had to be not only remote but also highly individual, their sole purpose being to provide a context for relaxation and the unadulterated enjoyment of arts,

culture and love. In other words, they were to be tiny oases of joie de vivre. It was thanks to this definition of purpose that they came to be called "pleasure castles" or "Maison de Plaisance" - a designation which covered hunting lodges as well.

Although King Friedrich II of Prussia, generally known as "Frederick the Great", had intended to make Charlottenburg (cf. Charlottenburg) his primary residence and had therefore set about enlarging it to meet his particular requirements, over the years, he found himself increasingly drawn to the tranquil little town of Potsdam. One year after planting a vineyard here in 1744, Friedrich abandoned his plans for Charlottenburg and instead began working on the fulfilment of a dream - his dream of henceforth living the life of a recluse in Potsdam, far away from the business and cares which had plagued him up until then. It was here that his court architect, Georg Wenzeslaus von Knobelsdorff, erected the wonderful summer residence which was to receive the name "Sans Souci", meaning "without cares". In Sanssouci, Friedrich could at last dedicate himself to his private pleasures and pastimes, was free to discourse, philosophize, make music, write poetry, ponder and compose.

Schloss Sanssouci, a genuine masterpiece of Rococco architecture, the vivacity and levity of which was much cherished in those days, was indeed a perfect setting for such activities, at least in the summer months. In winter however, Friedrich was obliged to abandon this jewel of a castle and its magnificent park in favour of Potsdam's Stadtschloss, which had a much better heating system.

Like many pleasure castles, Sanssouci consisted of a single-storey building with countless glass doors opening onto the garden almost at ground level. Just three steps separated the castle from the terraced vineyard, at the bottom of which there was a large pond. At that time, gardens were deemed to be just as important as the castle itself. The aim was to create as much harmony as possible between the work of man and the work of nature, the assumption being that even nature, like the universe itself, is governed by the rules of mathematics. Geometry and symmetry were thus the principles behind not only castle architecture but also garden architecture too.

The Baroque age was characterized by its love of clarity, logic, solid forms and transparent structures, set off by sensuousness and opulence coupled with a keen sense of ephemerality. Ancient Greece and Ancient Rome were still regarded as the golden age of culture, the intellectual, artistic, cultural and architectonic ideal to which all should aspire.

Frederick the Great too paid close attention to his estate. He made the park and castle more accessible by the addition of an avenue, 2.3 km long and flanked by several follies, pagodas, pavilions, temples, sculptures and bowers. The view from the castle was made still more awe-inspiring by the creation of a picturesque "point de vue", an artificial ruins with elements in the style of classical antiquity.

The interior of the castle was also heavily influenced by Italian motifs, especially in the so-called "Marble Room", where the dome and columns owe much to their classical models. The King's preference for French art is apparent in the east wing of the castle, which also contains the famous "Flower Chamber" - so called because of the flowers and birds with which it is so delightfully decorated. As Voltaire, the famous French writer and philosopher, is alleged to have stayed in this room on repeated occasions between 1750 and 1753, it is also known as the "Voltaire Room".

Neustadt-Glewe -
the sovereign prince's castle

This very grand, brick castle is still dominated by its huge keep. The top of this keep, however, was not added until the 16th century.

The castles of Mecklenburg-Western Pomerania are among the least visited and least researched of all those in Germany. In addition to the numerous small castles once owned by lesser nobles, two large, important castles, namely Stargard and Neustadt-Glewe, have also been respectably preserved. Nor is it by chance that both these castles belonged to the sovereign prince.

Such castles differed from those of the free or unfree nobility inasmuch as their architecture was generally more elaborate and impressive. Not only did they have to advertise the high social status of the lord, but also had to differentiate him from the rest of society by being bigger and grander than other castles and having excellent fixtures and furnishings. As the lord and his family were to reside there from time to time, they also had to offer a very high standard of residential comfort.

The castle gate is unusual in that it protrudes from the castle at a slight angle. It is flanked by the huge keep. Castle gates were often made to look especially splendid in order to impress in-coming visitors. In this case, it is both the gate and the keep which perform this function.

Furthermore, as administrative centres, they had to house both a steward and his personnel. This necessitated additional buildings as well as offices, storehouses and other utility buildings.

Castle Stargard, with its dense cluster of buildings, two gatehouses, castle church and spacious outer castle is an especially attractive example of such a large, sovereign prince's fortress.

The first fortifications in Neustadt were built by the Counts of Schwerin, then the Dukes of Mecklenburg, between 1225 and 1248 beside an important waterway. These were followed by a very pompous, brick castle built in the 14th and 15th centuries complete with a prominent, round keep to protect the adjacent castle gate on the south side of the building. The residential quarters and utility buildings are situated on the two shorter sides of the rectangular inner ward.

The castle as it stands today is the result of several rebuilding projects undertaken over the centuries, including the conversion work done around 1500 to accommodate artillery.

The castle is now fully restored and operational and attracts numerous visitors on account of its museum and cafeteria, its historical "Burgfest" held every year in the first week of June - to say nothing of various concerts and medieval banquets.

Celle -
a castle with two faces

The white castle which looks so homogeneous from afar is in fact the product of centuries of highly complicated building work, first begun in 1292. From 1530 to 1558, under Duke Ernst the Confessor, the castle became a splendid example of Renaissance architecture, of which only the east facade now remains. It was not until 1670 that the castle acquired the Baroque style it still has today.

Viewed from a distance, Schloss Celle appears to be a simple, four-sided structure with a polygonal tower at each corner and a plain, homogeneous roof. You have to be very close to the castle before the seven hundred years of building work that have gone into it become apparent.

It all began in the year 1292, when Duke Otto the Austere of Lüneburg realized that his castle, Burg (Alten)Celle, was situated in a rather inconvenient location. After all, just a few kilometres upstream, there was a sandy island which had once been the site of an old toll house and still marked the intersection of several trade routes. It was here, on this island in the river Aller, that Otto decided to erect his new castle, later to become Schloss Celle. The foundations of the huge, square tower which formed part of Otto's new seat, are still to be found inside today's castle, even if they are invisible from the outside.

After the Dukes of Lüneburg made Celle their primary residence in 1388, this tower was repeatedly enlarged over the decades which followed until Duke Friedrich the Pious turned it into an impressive castle at the end of the 15th century.

Schloss Celle became a masterpiece of early Renaissance architecture in 1530-58, under Duke Ernst the Confessor, who

View of the Baroque theatre inside the castle. This was installed on top of the walls of the oldest tower in the castle in 1674/75. It can hold 330 spectators while 55 more can be accommodated in the Studio. The interior of the theatre was the work of both Italian and German artists. Despite intensive restoration work between 1935 and 1938, the theatre has retained its original character and is now the oldest such theatre still in use in Germany.

opened up both castle and court to Renaissance influences. It was he who added the polygonal towers with their onion domes, just as it was he who divided up the facades with cornices, besides adding numerous tiny ornamental gables. His son, Duke Wilhelm the Younger, redesigned the late-Gothic chapel.

Nevertheless, this was by no means the last of the transformations Schloss Celle was to undergo. The castle acquired the appearance it still has today in 1670, under Duke Georg Wilhelm who, having been raised as a splendour-loving Baroque prince, had received his education in the great courts of France and Italy. The Duke summoned Italian artists and musicians, architects and craftsmen to his court and it was they who reworked three sides of the castle in the Baroque style. The east side of the castle, the side which faces the city and hence is the one most readily seen, was left untouched, for some reason. Yet it is precisely this east side of the castle which is the most admired and most photographed of them all.

Georg Wilhelm held the arts in such high esteem that he even installed a small, Baroque theatre in his castle - a theatre which is now deemed to be the oldest of its kind in Germany.

The 19th century saw the extensive levelling of the old fortifications and a transformation of the grounds into a romantic, English-style garden.

Dornröschenschloss Sababurg -
Sleeping Beauty's castle of Brothers Grimm fame

The Dornröschen-
schloss Sababurg
nestles idyllically
atop a basalt cone

in the heart of the
Reinhard Forest.
The huge great hall
with its two corner
towers topped with
bulbous cupolas still
gives us an idea of
the original size of
what used to be the
hunting lodge of
the landgraves of
Hesse.

After the Brothers Grimm published their collection of fairy-tales in the early 19th century, people began to refer to the ruined castle deep in the extensive Reinhard Forest as Sleeping Beauty's castle.

The history of this fairytale castle dates back to the years shortly before 1334, when the Archbishop of Mainz had a castle built on a prominent basalt cone in order to protect the shrine at Gottesbüren, an important place for pilgrimages. It was precisely this basalt cone, or "Zapfen", which gave the castle its original name of "Zappenborgk", which over the centuries gradually turned into the name it bears today.

The castle became famous as the probable site of Grimms' tale of the Sleeping Beauty: A spell cast by a witch caused life at the castle to freeze from one moment to the next. The

spell was not broken until a prince kissed the princess back to life, thus waking both her and her court and all the domestic animals from their 100-year sleep.

The Zappenborgk soon became a bone of contention between various territorial interests. In 1429, after the first division between Mainz and Hesse, the site passed to the landgraves of Hesse, who showed so little interest in the preservation of the castle, however, that it was soon afterwards described as "wüst", meaning "ruined".

The year 1490 marked the beginning of a better time for the desolate castle. It was then that the Landgrave Wilhelm I of Hesse had a great hall with two round towers built on the old foundations. This building was then enlarged by his son, Philipp I, so that by 1522, the castle had become a splendid hunting lodge, also used frequently for banquets and feasts. The two landgraves did not confine themselves to hunting, however, but also used the domain for their highly successful breeding of wild horses, the so-called "Sababurger Wilde".

In 1571, the Landgrave Wilhelm IV added a 125-hectare animal enclosure, the thorny hedges of which were replaced by a stone wall 2.5 metres high and 5 km long in the years 1590/92.

The Thirty Years' War caused the hunting lodge to go into decline. Repeatedly damaged in the course of the war, parts of the castle collapsed and it was even struck by lightning, meaning that it gradually turned into the dreamy, romantic, overgrown ruin so strikingly reminiscent of the setting of the miraculous tale of Sleeping Beauty.

From 1959 onwards, the Dornröschenschloss Sababurg, now 665 years old, was gradually kissed back to life. Today it houses a hotel, restaurant and café, a registry office and the SabaBurg Theatre in its late medieval, vaulted cellar. The outside of the castle with its decorative rose garden as well as a visit to the tower, the Grimm monument and romantic ruins will tell visitors a lot about its turbulent history.

In 1971, the animal enclosure was reopened and is now devoted to the preservation of rare species, once native to these parts. There is also a children's zoo and a museum of forestry and hunting. The "Urwald Sababurg", now a nature reserve which contains oak trees up to 1000 years old, is to be found nearby.

There are a number of atmospheric historical paintings of Sleeping Beauty's Castle still in existence. Unlike in the past, however, the castle is now easily accessible, especially as it is located on the "Deutsche Märchenstrasse", or German Fairytale Route.

Wilhelmshöhe -
nature dramatized

Cascading water-falls over 250 m long and interspersed with ponds and fountains rise up step by step from the castle to the summit. Here, the so-called "Giant Castle" is crowned by a pyramid which perpetuates the axial thrust of the cascades into the sky, leading up to a gigantic statue of Hercules. All this was part of a huge building project aimed at a three-dimensional "dramatization" of the Clash of the Titans of Greek mythology. The project was never actually completed.

The Wilhelmshöhe near Kassel has far more to offer than just a pyramid-crowned, "Giant Castle", visible for miles around. In reality, the castle itself is only the proverbial tip of the iceberg. From 1701 to 1718, two pleasure-loving and congenial Baroque personalities put their creative imagination and unharnessed dynamism to work on the realization of a sublime vision - the vision of a dramatized landscape. The man who commissioned the project, the Landgrave Karl of Hesse-Kassel, and his Italian architect, Giovanni Francesco Guerniero, wanted to render Europe's courts speechless with astonishment and reverence for a truly spectacular architectural project consisting of nothing less than a three-dimensional realization of the much-admired Clash of the Titans from Greek mythology.

The site they chose for this "dramatization" was a steep hill in the Habichtswald, which was given the name Karlsberg. Their plan envisaged a splendid park spread over a wide terrace, at the centre of which there was to be a pompous palace in the style of a villa. From here, there was to be a series of cascades and ponds leading up to the top of the hill, which in turn was to be crowned with yet another magnificent castle. And these first plans did not even include the famous pyramid!

In actual fact, only the tip of the iceberg was ever completed - namely the "Giant Castle" on the summit and the breathtaking cascades with their large, statue-studded ponds, grottos and enormous fountains. The addition of the pyramid was a stroke of genius that led to a bizarre and dramatic continuation of the cascades up into the sky. The pyramid itself supported a 9-metre-high copper Hercules, resting casually on his huge cudgel and looking utterly bored by the trivial busybodying of the mortal world below. Naturally, many princes loved to be identified and equated with divine heroes and it goes without saying that Hercules too, was not put in such a dominant position by chance. In the age of absolutism, princes and kings ruled very much like omnipotent deities, plundering their own people in order to satisfy their boundless craving for glory. The gigantic statue of Hercules alone, whose very cudgel had space for eight people (!), cost the Landgrave Karl a small fortune.

The vision was eventually completed by two other landgraves. Friedrich II (1760-85) had a romantic park added in the English style while Wilhelm IX (1790-98) built a splendid castle at the foot of the waterfalls. The romanticism of the castle garden was enhanced still further by the addition of two follies: a ruined "Roman" aquaduct complete with its own waterfall and a large, ruined castle called the Löwenburg.

View of the landgrave's bathroom inside Schloss Wilhelmshöhe. The antique pastoral motifs painted on the wooden panelling were not added until 1825, as was the marble basin inspired by Ancient Egypt. The classical castle was built between 1791 and 1798 under Landgrave Wilhelm IX and now houses an important collection of interior furnishings and paintings.

Marburg -
the rediscovered castle of the Thuringians

View of the historical part of the town and castle with the Wilhelmsbau (right) and the chapel (centre). Thanks to the landgraves of Thuringia, both the town and castle were closely associated with St Elisabeth, who set up a hospital here before her death in 1231 at the tender age of 24. The early Gothic church of St Elisabeth was built on her grave.

The landgraves of Thuringia built a castle on the Schlossberg in Marburg to secure their lordship claims even before 1138/39. This castle was replaced by a new building in the 13th century and, because no visible remains were left standing, was thought to have vanished completely. All the greater, therefore, was the astonishment in August 1989 when the excellently well preserved bottom half of a much older castle was discovered during building work underneath the West Wing. The remains found were part of a fortified house dating from around 1000 A.D., reduced to a residential tower towards the end of the 11th century and finally used merely for the static stabilization of the

View of the south side of the castle with the chapel of St Katharina, first consecrated in 1288. The windows and oriels are late Gothic and Renaissance additions.

Paintings in the so-called "Gedächtnisraum" or "Hall of Memory", intended to commemorate the theological debate between Luther and Zwingli, held here in the year 1529 at the instigation of the Landgrave Philipp.

much larger superstructures built on top of it. But at least now, the original castle of the Thuringians is once again visible through a hole in the floor - complete with its walls 6 metres high!

During the centuries to follow, the castle was repaired, rebuilt and enlarged until, in the course of the late 15th and 16th centuries, it became a very beautiful residential castle at which numerous landgraves of Hesse chose to reside. The splendid Gothic interiors with their vaulted ceilings, above all the magnificent "Fürstensaal" and wonderful chapel, consecrated by St Katharina in 1288, were among the first parts of the castle to be improved. It is the spirit of late Gothicism, on the other hand, which is apparent in the bowers, meaning the West Wing and the Wilhelmsbau.

And just as the castle was transformed into a palace, so it also became a fortress: After a huge battery tower was built in 1478, the fortifications were upgraded during the chaotic years of the Thirty Years' War - i.e. around 1620 - and later around 1700/10, by the addition of bastions, casemates, hornworks and outer entrenchments, all of which made it a powerful stronghold with which to protect the town. It did not hold out long, however, for in 1807, Napoleon ordered the destruction of all the fortifications.

After the 19th century had allowed the castle to degenerate into a prison, it finally underwent cautious restoration work in 1972-81, thanks to which it once again became a jewel of Gothicism. Even parts of the fortifications have since been exposed and restored by the town.

Goslar -
the most famous residence in the Reich

View of the front of the "Kaiserpfalz" in Goslar, whose present condition is thanks largely to the restoration work of 1868-79. The numerous arcade windows indicate the old "Kaisersaal" or aula regis on the first floor, which used to be accessible via an outside staircase. This feature must have been added in the course of the 12th century, however. Today, the palace is considered a valuable example of secular, Romanesque architecture.

View of the 13th century tomb of Kaiser Heinrich III (died 1056) in St Ulrich's chapel. In accordance with his will, the kaiser's heart was buried beneath this monument to demonstrate his sense of allegiance to Goslar. The chapel, built in the early 12th century, was used as an advocate's jail from 1289 onwards.

It has often been said that the German Kaisers of the Early and High Middle Ages ruled their crown lands from the back of a horse. Although this is somewhat exaggerated, it is indeed true to say that they were peripatetic rulers, who governed and administered the Reich from several palaces, the so-called "Kaiserpfalzen", spread throughout the country. As all the kaisers visited their favourite palaces more frequently and for longer periods than the others, some of these imperial palaces were furnished more elaborately and comfortably than others.

Shortly before 1017, political considerations induced Kaiser Heinrich II to abandon his Pfalz Werla in favour of a new building in Goslar. Although the imperial silver mines had made this town a prosperous economic centre, it was nevertheless at risk from the riotous Saxons. It was not until the reign of Heinrich's successor, Konrad II (1024-1038) and above all that of Heinrich III (1038-1056), however, that the palace still in existence today came into being.

No fewer than 23 sessions of the exalted imperial court were held within these walls. Kaiser Heinrich III visited Goslar, his

View of the restored "Kaisersaal"
with historical
paintings by Hermann Wislicenus
dating from 1879-97.
The paintings were
intended to depict
both the glory of the
Holy Roman Empire and that of the
new German Empire. The dimensions of the hall

favourite Pfalz, twenty-two times, while Kaiser Heinrich IV (1056-1106) paid thirty visits.

Despite its outstanding importance, the imperial palace in Goslar appears to have been jinxed: Not only did it burn down in the year 1065 but in 1107, it was struck by lightning, which allegedly damaged the Kaiser's sword and shield leaning against his bed. In 1132, parts of the palace collapsed during the a session of the imperial court, crushing several people, and in 1289, or so a contemporary reported, a fire razed the imperial palace to the "grunt", i.e. to the foundations. Although the town began the necessary reconstruction work just one year later, other palaces had long since come to overshadow that at Goslar.

By the end of the Middle Ages, little of the great palace described so enthusiastically and as early as 1077/78 by the historian, Lampert of Hersfeld, as "the most famous residence in the Reich" and "home and hearth" of the German kings, was still in existence.

give visitors of good
idea of how impressive this building
must have been
back in the 11th or
12th centuries,
when the German
kings actually resided here.

When part of the neglected ruins of the imperial palace in Goslar collapsed in 1865, the Hannoverian government had the building restored and the "Kaisersaal", at the express wish of the Kaiser, decorated with paintings glorifying scenes from German history by Hermann Wislicenus. In the years of patriotic euphoria which followed, the palace regained at least part of its former glory as a new, or rather rediscovered, monument and is now considered an important example of secular, Romanesque architecture.

Little is known, however, about the palace which used to stand on this site, built under Kaiser Heinrich II in 1015. The foundations uncovered to the east of the imperial palace during excavation work in 1886/87 doubtless belong to this earlier building.

Ahaus -
reminiscent of the Middle Ages

View of the front side of the island castle. After being destroyed during the Second World War, the splendid Baroque castle was carefully restored and is now the seat of the Technical Academy of Ahaus. It has also gained fame as a venue for concerts, which have been a regular feature here since 1952.

Westphalia still has an impressively wide range of excellently well preserved island castles. This special type of castle is characteristic of low-lying, often water-logged land and is therefore encountered frequently in the Netherlands, Belgium and parts of Scandinavia as well. These island castles are always built in the middle of a broad moat, pond or lake and are usually remarkable for the simplicity of their architecture. This is because unlike hill-top castles, whose shape and structure had to be adapted to the prevailing topography, the flat sites on which island castles were built did not subject their builders to any kind of spatial restrictions. It was therefore possible to build these castles as planned.

The gatehouse of the castle contains a small museum with numerous archaeological finds, including luxury items belonging to the household of the prince bishop and examples of local craftsmanship. Among these are items of faience porcelain made at the local faience manufactory. The late medieval leather shoes retrieved in the course of an archaeological dig and well preserved thanks to the dampness of the soil are also well worth seeing.

This, of course, was an ideal state of affairs for the builders of Renaissance and Baroque palaces, who preferred clearly organized, geometrical structures.

One outstanding example of such a castle is Schloss Ahaus, built in 1689-95 as a residence for the Prince Bishop of Münster, Friedrich Christian von Plettenberg, in Flemish Baroque style.

The basic outline of this three-winged building is remarkable for its meticulous symmetry, its two main gates being situated on an imaginary central axis which is further enhanced by the central gable of the main building. The two wings end in tower-like pavilions, which in turn lend the front facade its monumental impact.

The palace is at the centre of a walled, rectangular island with a pavilion at each corner. The main gate in the middle of the front side is likewise flanked by two more pavilions.

The shrewd positioning of these pavilions makes Ahaus vaguely reminiscent of a concentric medieval castle. Architectural elements such as towers, embrasures, drawbridges, ditches, battlements and corbelled turrets had long since served to illustrate what had traditionally been a privilege of the nobility - namely the right to build castles. After the Middle Ages, therefore, the builders of palaces such as Ahaus often included these features as a means of alluding to and reviving the glorious days of chivalry.

In the case of Ahaus, there was some justification for this historicism, because there had indeed been a medieval castle on this very site, which in 1406 passed into the hands of the bishopric and was destroyed completely to make way for the new palace. This is evident from the incredibly precise symmetry of both the island and the palace itself.

Vischering -
an old castle on a man-made island

Most Westphalian island castles date back to the Renaissance and Baroque eras. Unlike these symmetrically designed, somewhat matter-of-fact castles, the picturesque Wasserburg Vischering has an attractive round shape and this fact alone is proof of its older origins.

Indeed, it was built shortly before 1271 by the Bishop of Münster, who needed it to protect his territory against the expansionism of the neighbouring lordships. The structure he chose consisted of a high curtain wall, encircling a small, oval-shaped inner ward. This ward contained a number of residential buildings and utility buildings as well as a kind of tower, as was discovered during an archaeological work on the castle. A narrow wooden bridge led to the large outer castle, also situated on a man-made island, which in turn was connected to the "mainland" by a drawbridge. Both the outer castle and main castle were originally protected by additional ditches and walls.

The building of an island castle was no easy undertaking. The first job was to drive countless oak piles deep into the san-

This dreamy island castle is the result of the rebuilding which took place after a fire in 1521 and subsequent conversion work. Its round shape, however, is a clear pointer to its 13th century origins. It is still owned by the von Droste family.

dy riverbed at a shallow point in the river. These piles were then used to support the masonry, which naturally had to be watertight. To achieve this, castle-builders used to mix their mortar with brick dust. Once the building work was finished, the river was rechannelled in such a way that both the outer castle and the main castle formed islands in the middle of a wide river. It was vital for the piles to remain wet, as otherwise

View of the west side. The brickwork shows where the old stone wall had to be patched up when the late 13th century curtain wall was raised and windows added. Today, the castle houses a cultural centre and the Coesfeld District Museum.

they would begin to rot and crumble. This is why the lowering of ground-water levels often severely damages island castles and other structures built on wet foundations.

This happened to Vischering after two extremely dry summers in 1911/12. Huge cracks began to appear in the facades and there were fears that the walls might break apart. It was not until 1927-29, when a concrete wreath and star-shaped, reinforced concrete anchor which clamped the walls together were added, that the castle on the verge of bursting at the seams regained its static equilibrium. Life was much more difficult for medieval builders: Any buildings in danger of collapsing had to be dismantled brick by brick, the foundations remade and the entire building rebuilt, or enormous support structures installed.

After a fire in 1521, the next few decades saw the castle transformed into a more homely dwelling, without losing its original layout, however. Indeed, parts of the old curtain wall have been preserved. Other rebuilding projects, such as that at Ahaus, began by removing all previous structures so thoroughly that no trace of their existence remained.

Fortunately, the bombs which rained down during the Second World War did not inflict any serious damage. In 1971, the District of Coesfeld leased the castle so that it could be used as a cultural centre. During the renovation work, some rare secco paintings from the 16th century were discovered in the "Rittersaal". Today, the castle houses a museum and a restaurant.

Stolzenfels -
toll house and prince's castle

Stolzenfels was the first ruined castle on the Rhine to be "restored" by the Prussian royal family. What Schinkel and - after his death

in 1841 - his pupil, Friedrich August Stüler, created here is a masterpiece of historicism.

The interior of the castle in particular was used for an especially lavish display of the owners' pomp and splendour. The neo-Gothic interiors had to accommodate valuable, exquisite collections of paintings, furniture, weapons, statuettes and other objets d'art. One of the many highlights of a tour of the castle is the king's living room, which contains a superb writing desk dated around 1700.

The yellow walls of Burg Stolzenfels look down majestically on the Rhine within sight of the city of Koblenz. The highly ornate silhouette of the castle, with its countless towers, turrets, oriels and battlements, is a clear sign to anyone who knows about castles that this is another of the 19th century's pseudo-historical creations. Yet Stolzenfels has a special place among the Rhine's numerous neo-Gothically rebuilt castles, because together with the nearby Burg Rheinstein, it is Stolzenfels which marks the beginning of the romantic Rhine Gorge.

In 1823, the city of Koblenz gave the abandoned ruins to the Prussian crown prince and later King Friedrich Wilhelm IV as a present. The Rhine had long since become the most Germanic of Germany's rivers, a cult river immortalized in many a saga and final resting place of the famous Nibelungen treasure - to say nothing of its legendary castles. The Prussian royal family, however, saw the reconstruction of the ruined castle as a unique opportunity to revive the power and glory of days gone by while at the same time putting the aspiring masses back in their place - at least symbolically.

Just two years later, in 1825, Prince Friedrich Ludwig of Prussia, a nephew of King Friedrich Wilhelm, bought the ruined Burg Rheinstein in order to have a pendant to the new Burg Stolzenfels.

From the mid-19th century onwards, scarcely any of the Rhine castles was spared this kind of programmatic restyling, as one rich commoner or industrialist after another sought to imitate the nobility and upgrade his social status by buying, "restoring" or rebuilding castles. Unlike in the Middle Ages when the right to own a castle was a privilege of the nobility, castles now became the ultimate status symbol for all echelons of society and visible proof of successful social climbing.

Around 1900, Kaiser Wilhelm II linked the rebuilding of castles to the imperial ideology by having the Hohkönigsburg in Alsace restored in monumental style as the western cornerstone of the Reich. This actually returned castles to their original purpose: Once again, their primary purpose was to demonstrate power and claims to hegemony.

Friedrich Wilhelm's main concern was likewise a manifestation of power. He therefore commissioned the famous architect, Karl Friedrich Schinkel, with the resurrection of the castle originally built around 1250 as a toll house for the Archbishopric of Trier like the phoenix from the ashes.

Cochem -
"sacrificed to Vulcan in broad daylight"

The extraordinarily picturesque silhouette of Burg Cochem is the result of its romantic restoration between 1868 and 1879, when it was both enlarged and adorned with countless turrets. The keep still dominates the castle, however, just as it would have done in the Middle Ages.

The Rhine and Moselle are world famous for their picturesque castles and palaces. The fact that most of these did not acquire the picturesque appearance they enjoy today until the 19th century is common knowledge. Nevertheless, many visitors consider these castles to be "authentic" copies of medieval castles, not realizing that they have more to do with the 18th and 19th century imagination than the real Middle Ages. Among the castles in this category is the pretty Burg Cochem which, with its numerous towers and turrets, is one of the most frequently photographed landmarks of the wine-growing Moselle valley.

View of the so-called "Hunting Room" which imitates a late Gothic interior, despite the Renaissance furniture it contains. The painted window panes enhance the picturesque quality of this room. The

Like nearly all castles rebuilt in the 19th century, Burg Cochem was built on the site of a medieval castle which, after being modified and added to over the centuries, finally disappeared inside the romantic stage-set erected in 1874-1877.

Originally a very old imperial castle, Cochem passed to the Archbishop of Trier in 1294. The fact that the church coveted such castles was by no means unusual in those days, when the church was an important pillar of secular, and not just ecclesiastical power. It was the clerics who were involved in politics, who built castles, installed territories, secured claims to lordship, led military campaigns, accumulated land and other property, engaged in intrigue as well as cleansing the earth of heretics and even getting into quarrels with the kaisers.

19th century had a completely distorted view of what life in a medieval castle was like - as is evident here from the luxurious nature of the interior. Such a high level of comfort, however, was not to be had in most castles - where the residential quarters were usually rather poor and spartan.

Replica of a 16th century suit of armour. The pointed iron hat was superseded by the bucket-like helmet in the 12th and 13th centuries. Over the years, this bucket-like helmet was modified to produce a variety of helmets, including those with a drop-down vizor. The various parts of the body were protected by iron plates.

until she confessed. Those who did not confess were assumed to be possessed by the devil and hence guilty no matter what they pleaded! In other words, whether a "witch" confessed or not, she was bound to end up being burnt at the stake. Especially gruesome and above all completely unfair was the so-called "Test by Water", which involved immersing the recalcitrant suspect in water. If she survived this or if her dead body floated to the surface of the water, she was obviously guilty. If, however, her body sank to the bottom, she was innocent. The reasoning behind this absurd procedure was that as the baptism of Christ had rendered all water holy, it would of course reject the presence of a criminal.

The witch-hunters were feared wherever they went, especially as they went about their work with great zeal, often applying sexual pressure and intimidation to obtain their grisly results.

It was in the decades around 1600 that the Inquisition committed its worst excesses. Thank God it went into decline thereafter - although the last witches were burned to death as late as the mid-18th century. It is estimated that over 100,000 people throughout Europe lost their lives as a result of the Inquisition, only ten per cent of whom were men.

Among the buildings added to the castle in the 14th century under the Archbishop Balduin of Trier is the so-called "Witch's Tower", which keeps watch over the gate to the main castle. Names such as "Witch's Tower", "Thief's Tower", "Prison Tower", "Torture Tower" etc. were given mainly to the towers of urban fortifications when they were requisitioned for use as prisons by the Inquisition or when the romantics identified them as the scene of epic sagas.

The Inquisition began in the late 15th century when the church, under the influence of Pope Innocent VIII's bull of 1484 authorizing the persecution of witches and the "Witches' Hammer" which appeared three years later, began ferreting out the witches in its midst. By 1669, the notorious "Witches' Hammer", which described in great detail how to identify witches and how best to stamp them out, had been reprinted no fewer than 29 times and was regarded as the witch-hunter's bible.

As the condemned person's property was confiscated by the church, the Inquisition soon proved to be a highly lucrative business - including for judges, jurors and informers, all of whom received commissions. Furthermore, it also became a convenient way of getting rid of unwelcome competition, meaning herbalists, midwives, wise women, miracle healers and free thinkers, all of whom were branded as heretics.

Those who landed in the town's witch's house, witch's tower or, worse still, in the torture chamber, stood little chance of survival. If the charged was denied, the suspect was tortured

Replica of a 16th century suit of armour. As warriors, knights had to be especially well protected. Suits of chain mail which covered the whole body were available from the 12th century onwards. Despite this, the cross-bow and heavy lances necessitated increasingly heavy armour.

Replica of the 2.3-metre-high suit of armour belonging to the court giant of Innsbruck, Giovanni Bona, from the 16th century, kept at Schloss Ambras near Innsbruck. He must have had to carry an incredible weight on his body when wearing full battle dress.

This all changed in 1868 when the councillor of commerce, Jakob Louis Ravené purchased the ruins from the Prussian administration. Fascinated by the restoration projects already under way on many a neighbouring castle, he decided to rebuild the ruined Burg Cochem in late Gothic style. Although much of the building work was based on historical views of the castle dating from the 16th and 17th centuries, Ravené deliberately modified the original by the addition of new superstructures, miniature battlements and slim turrets, in order to lend it as romantic a silhouette as possible. The interiors of the newly installed residential and service buildings were not based on any specific models and so covered a wide range of styles. The castle was also used to house a museum with various historical exhibits.

Among the numerous legends to recur in a number of different places along the Rhine and Moselle and which are completely without any kind of historical basis is that concerning an iron chain, allegedly used to block the river Moselle and levy tolls at the foot of Burg Cochem. The same is often said of the famous "Mouse Tower" in the middle of the Rhine near Bingen. The fact is, however, the breadth of the river and strong, almost raging currents, to say nothing of the weight of the chain which would have necessitated a gigantic tensioning mechanism and huge anchors, neither of which was available on either the Rhine or the Moselle.

After being damaged during the Second World War, the castle was purchased by the town of Cochem in 1978 and is now opened to guided tours as well as housing a restaurant.

Despite this appalling record, the late 18th and 19th centuries adopted names such as "Witch's Tower" and "Torture Tower" with great enthusiasm, as these were very much in keeping with their image of the Middle Ages as a dark and bloodthirsty era. The High Middle Ages, however, to which most of our castles belong, actually built its towers with much more peaceful purposes in mind. Most of them were symbols of power and lordship, rarely equipped with dungeons and fortified only up to a point. It is thus no surprise that Cochem's "Witch's Tower" had nothing to do with witches originally.

Whereas Cochem survived the Thirty Years' War (1618-48) more or less unscathed, the decades which followed brought still more calamity and suffering for both the castle and the town of Cochem. It was then that the French invaded the Palatinate and seized military control of the Rhine. Not only was the Palatinate itself laid waste but in 1689, nearly all the castles on the Rhine and Moselle, in the Hunsrück and Eifel, went up in flames. The turn of Burg Cochem came on May 19, 1689. It was on this day that the French, having contented themselves sixteen years previously with a few cannonballs tossed in the direction of the castle, finally decided to burn it down. For three days, "Vulcan" raged and whatever was left over after this three-day inferno was promptly undermined and blasted. The town of Cochem, which at this time was defended by imperial troops, suffered a similar fate on August 25/26: The French stormed the town, butchered both soldiers and civilians alike and then set fire to what was left - a catastrophe from which the town recovered only very slowly, while the castle was left to go to ruin.

Replica of a 16th century suit of armour. In the 15th and 16th centuries, knights were completely protected by their armour. Despite this, the arquebus could penetrate even this type of armour and pikes could be used to dismount the horseback warriors. The increasing popularity of tournaments led to the introduction of special tilting armour which could be very splendid and showy indeed. This armour, however, soon came to be used for representative purposes only, as numerous, very glamourous suits of armour show.

Trifels -
where Richard the Lionheart was held captive

In the 12th and 13th centuries, Trifels, located on a steep, unassailable rock, 300 m above and valley bottom, in the middle of Reich territory and surrounded by other imperial castles, was considered one of the safest places in the Reich. It was for this reason that the crown jewels, including the imperial crown, sceptre, orb, sword and cross, were all kept here, as were such prominent captives as the English King Richard the Lionheart, who was imprisoned here in 1192/93.

During the Third Crusade, the English King, often described as arrogant and dictatorial, had insulted Duke Leopold of Austria so seriously that the duke had sworn revenge. When King Richard returned from the Holy Land, a storm obliged him to take a different route home and to pass through Austria, disguised as a merchant. Once he was unmasked, however,

The reasons behind Kaiser Heinrich VI's decision to hold his English counterpart captive at Trifels were rather less chivalrous: The need to finance an expensive war against the rebellious Italians had left him with a serious liquidity problem. Thanks to the ransom obtained, however, he was able to return home not just victorious but also in possession of the Norman crown jewels, transported to Trifels on no fewer than 150 pack-animals.

The conspicuous Trifels rock was inhabited even in the last few centuries B.C.. Evidence of a 10th century wooden fortress has been found, as have remains of a stone castle with roughcast walls, built in the second half of the 11th century, probably by the Salian kings. Around 1200, the Hohenstaufens erected an impressive new castle on the same site, the importance of which, however, steadily declined after the end of the Hohenstaufen era (1268).

View of the small hall. Inside the castle, a number of rooms have retained their original Hohenstaufen appearance - among them the chapel, the apse of which once formed the oriel of a residential tower. Other rooms, including the "Kaisersaal" in the new great hall, were rebuilt between 1938 and 1954. The monumental architecture of the new great hall is symptomatic of the efforts of the Nazi regime to turn Trifels into a national monument.

Duke Leopold wasted no time in having him incarcerated in Burg Dürnstein in the Wachau. Kaiser Heinrich VI, however, persuaded the vengeful duke to hand the prisoner over to him so that he could extort a ransom for his release. As King Philipp II August of France was just as anxious to "buy" the arch-enemy he so despised as the English were to rescue him, Richard's ransom continued to climb to astronomical heights, until the English finally succeeded in outbidding the French.

Then there is the touching, but historically unsubstantiated tale of the singer, Blondel, who in 1193 set off for Germany with the intention of bringing his sovereign lord and master back home. Blondel travelled from castle to castle until he finally reached Trifels, where the unmistakably sonorous voice of his king suddenly and unexpectedly joined in the song he was singing. The loyal and courageous Blondel later returned to the castle accompanied by twelve knights who liberated Richard that very night.

It was the age of Romanticism which rediscovered Trifels as Germany's very own "Castle of the Holy Grail" and a great monument to Hohenstaufen architecture. The legends of King Arthur and the Knights of the Round Table were very popular at that time, as is proven by the huge success of Richard Wagner's operas, "Parsifal" and "Lohengrin". Yet the castle which kept the Holy Grail - the vessel in which the blood of Jesus was collected after his crucifixion - had a special role to play as a divine dream castle, as the castle to end all castles, even in the Arthurian legends of the 13th and 14th century. The search for the Castle of the Holy Grail which was the original quest of the Knights of the Round Table, was taken up again with renewed enthusiasm in the 19th century.

The Nazis also saw in Trifels an ideal symbol of Germany's former power, glory and strength and in 1938-42 therefore had it rebuilt in a bombastic style.

During the age of Romanticism, the grand and imposing Burg Trifels was described as Germany's Castle of the Holy Grail. Yet Trifels had been an important imperial castle as far back as the High Middle Ages. The old castle was renovated around 1200 and a large residential tower with an integrated chapel and beautiful hall added. The great hall was then built onto the existing buildings. An arcade connected the well tower at the front with the rest of the castle. The monumental appearance the castle has today is the result of its restyling in 1938-42 and 1963-66.

Marksburg -
Rhenish hill-top castle in Japan

The Marksburg towers proudly over the Rhine valley. The only serious damage it ever suffered was that inflicted by the Second World War. Today, it is home to the German Castles Association, which is currently in the process of having it rerendered. The Great Battery with the advocate's tower is visible on the left, with the inner castle to the right, the slim keep in the centre and chapel tower on the far right.

Situated majestically high up above the pretty little town of Braubach on the right bank of the Rhine is a castle called the Marksburg. The pride and power demonstrated by its cliff-top location make this castle far more worthy of the name "Stolzenfels", meaning "proud rock", than the castle which really does bear that name, visible further downstream. The Marksburg claims to be the "only undestroyed hill-top castle on the Rhine," although it has far more to offer than just this: Since 1900, it has been home to the Deutsche Burgenvereinigung [German Castles Association], Germany's oldest grassroots movement for the preservation of historical buildings and a trustee of the Institute of European Castles. It was here that Bodo Ebhardt, founder of the association and one of Germany's most important castle experts, lived, worked and died. It was here that one of the world's most extensive libraries on the subject of castles

The Great Battery was completed in two sections: It started out as a small gun house in the early 16th century and was enlarged to its present size in 1743-45. This gun emplacement made it possible to control shipping on the Rhine. Until then, the only military purpose of the castle had been to protect the silver mines.

emerged over the years just as it is still here, in fact more than ever before, that the nerve centre of German castle research is to be found.

The Marksburg was not the first castle to be built on this site. Its predecessor, however, located near Braubach's parish church of St Martin, has all but disappeared. Despite this, the mention of a "Schloss Braubach" in a document dating from the year 1231, is almost certainly a reference to the Marksburg, which at that time was enfeoffed by the Count Palatine to the Lords of Eppstein and was already known to be a highly profitable demesne owing to the right to collect tolls.

Some fifty years later, the town of Braubach and the Marksburg passed to the influential Counts of Katzenelnbogen, who immediately set about inducing King Albrecht to grant them the right to start mining for silver and other metals within one mile of Schloss Braubach and as far as the banks of the Rhine. This silver mining turned out to be a highly lucrative sideline

from which the Marksburg also profited, given that its fortifications had to be reinforced in order to protect the mine.

Whereas the Counts of Hesse, the new lords of the manor until 1645, transformed the Marksburg into a fortress in keeping with the times, in the century that followed, it degenerated into a home for invalids and state prison.

When Bodo Ebhardt bought the castle for the Deutsche Burgenvereinigung from the Prussian government in 1900, he had already decided not only to restore the Marksburg to its original, late-medieval appearance, but also to transform it into an "ideal German castle". Ebhardt's restoration of the Hohkönigsburg, Burg Kipfenberg and the Veste Coburg had already earned him the reputation of Germany's greatest architect and castle expert. The pomposity of Ebhardt's restorations and his obsession with fortifications meant that his work was not viewed uncritically even then. It is here that Ebhardt's very personal view of castles becomes apparent. For him, castles were above all war-oriented, demonstrations of power. As his newly completed reconstruction of the Hohkönigsburg had provided the German empire with a splendid cornerstone, much to the satisfaction of the man who commissioned it, namely no lesser person than the Kaiser Wilhelm II himself, the Kaiser's protegé managed to survive these attacks on his achievements unscathed. He was therefore able to furnish the Marksburg not only with an impressive Great Hall, but also with bowers, huge wine cellars, a large kitchen, an armory and the inevitable torture chamber. The interior was medievalized and the chapel painted "in the style of the first half of the 15th century". To ensure that visitors to the castle could be received in a befitting manner, Ebhardt even added a new drawbridge to the gatehouse.

Bodo Ebhardt died in 1945, and was thus spared the pain of seeing "his" castle seized and severely damaged by American troops. The years which followed were spent on tedious repair and restoration work, which also yielded a lot of new findings with regard to the Marksburg's architectural history.

Despite this, the precise history of how the Marksburg came into being is still unclear. Romanesque remains have repeatedly been found in the core of the castle, indicating that it was first built in the 13th century. The small, slim keep probably dates from this period as well. The extensive outer bailey with its towers and embrasures was not added until 1440, according to the latest research, this being the year in which the castle was first enlarged. Nor did work on the castle stop after the first gun emplacements were installed in the 16th century. The outer bastions with the prominent "sharp corner", completed in 1643-45, are younger still.

Today, the Marksburg is once again an intact and most attractive castle, further enriched by the "medieval" herb garden added in 1969. Its charms also attracted the attention of an

The Great Hall
was added in 1900
by the castle enthu-
siast, Bodo Ebhardt.
This tastefully fur-
nished, bright,
warm and comfor-
table hall shows us
how he imagined
the lords of the
manor to have
lived. As the
Marksburg was
never particularly
important in the
Middle Ages, how-
ever, those who in-
habited it probably
had to endure con-
siderable hardship
and privation. Few
of the rooms could
be heated and win-
dow glass was both
extremely expensive
and hard to come
by. During the win-
ter months, it was
dark and sooty in-
side the castle and
never more than
luke-warm - assum-
ing, of course, there
was a fire in the
hearth.

enterprising Japanese municipality, which has since had a life-size reproduction of the Marksburg built on the island of Okinawa Miyako.

This curiosity has not impaired the original Marksburg's value as a tourist attraction, however. On the contrary, as a number of Japanese tourists now want to visit the original castle, a miniature railway has been built to transport visitors from the river up to the castle.

Ever since ghosts were sighted in the chapel tower in 1932, Marksburg pilgrims have also included ghost enthusiasts. On what, regrettably, is a rather poorly focussed photograph of the chapel window taken in that year, it suddenly became possible to make out the outline of a person at prayer. Now of course there are thousands of ghost stories surrounding Germany's castles. Some of the motifs, including the woman in white, the sad virgin and the treasury guarded by a flaming dog, have become almost obligatory. Especially popular are those stories which seek to explain why a certain castle was built in a cer-tain place (like the Wartburg). Castle sites usually seem to be chosen on account of some miraculous rescue or recovery alleged to have occurred there. Sadly, there is rarely more than a hint of truth in these tales. After all, castles have always proved especially inspiring to the human imagination.

The inside of the castle is accessible to guided tours only, but is well worth a visit, if only to see Ebhardt's interior decor.

Eltz -
eight towers on a postage stamp

The world famous Burg Eltz attracts countless visitors from all corners of the globe year in year out, despite its remote location. Indeed, it is not just the castle's picturesque walls and towers, but also the desolate, romantic valley in which it is situated which make this castle so fascinating - calling to mind our childhood images of knights in shining armour and damsels in distress.

Yet Burg Eltz has far more to offer than just romantic cloud-capped towers and is far more than just a hollow tourist attraction. Not only is it a "genuine" castle, but it also has a most interesting and unusual history. Although both the 19th and 20th centuries spruced up this rather delapidated castle both inside and out, added a detail or two here and there and retouched some of the paintwork, by great good fortune, the basic shape of this "multi-family castle" was left untouched.

Like nearly all the castles described here, it took several centuries for Burg Eltz, which began life as a modest residential tower, to turn into the complex and impressive castle it is today. The original tower, also known as the "Platteltz" and built in 1157 by the kaiser's liegeman, Rudolph of Eltz, is now to be found at the southern end of the castle, together with the ground floor residential quarters belonging to it, the so-called "House of Kempenich".

In 1268, the family split into three main lines and the castle had to be shared between them. Eltz therefore became a so-called "Ganerbenburg" or multi-family castle, in which peace treaties agreed between the residents or communities of heirs helped keep the peace within the complex. Yet many centuries were to pass before the castle acquired the shape it takes today. It was not until the 15th, 16th and early 17th centuries that the "Rübenach Tower", "Grossrodendorf Tower", "Kleinrodendorf Tower" and "Kempenich Tower" were built, all of which gave rise to an architectural conglomerate made up of eight towers with nearly 100 residential rooms and completely enclosing the small inner ward.

Among the most important members of the influential and well-endowed Eltz family were Jacob of Eltz (1510-81), who became Elector and Archbishop of Trier, and above all Philipp Karl, who became Elector of Mainz in 1732.

Thanks to the diplomatic acumen of its owners, Burg Eltz managed to survive all the major wars undamaged and is still owned by the Eltz family even today. The only hard times it ever had to endure were in the years 1331-33.

It was then that the Elector Balduin of Trier - a cunning power politician and a great castle builder - attempted to pacify his electorate. This, of course, instantly brought him into conflict with the free nobles, who believed their right to feuds to be in jeopardy. In those days, the feud was still a time-honoured privilege of the nobility - a privilege which enabled them to settle their internal differences by the sword. On June 15, 1331, the free knights formed an alliance and solemnly undertook to come to each other's aid together with 50, heavily armed knights in the event of war.

Understandably enough, Balduin interpreted this as a provocation and immediately set about disbanding the alliance by force. That same year, he advanced on Burg Eltz, but found it to be so well fortified that he had a small fortress erected on the neighbouring hill - Burg Baldeneltz, also known as Trutzeltz - from which he could besiege it.

The castle is located in a remote, romantic spot on a bend in the river Eltz. Most of its picturesque towers and oriels were added in the 15th and 16th centuries, when it had to accommodate several families. This building work resulted in a dense conglomerate of eight residential towers with over 100 rooms. The view from the north shows the Rodendorf Houses at the front and the Rübenach House to the right with the "Platteltz" tower, the oldest part of the castle, behind it.

Burg Baldeneltz not only overlooked Burg Eltz but unfortunately was also close enough to attack it with catapulted or thrown missiles. After two tortuous years of living under a shower of heavy stone balls and cut off from their supply lines, the castle occupants were finally sufficiently demoralized to abandon the castle. On January 9, 1336, the "Peace Treaty of Eltz" was signed, as a result of which the free knights of Eltz became vassals of the elector. This meant that Burg Baldeneltz, which in 1337 was also described as the "Nuwe Eltz", belonged to them, even though they showed little interest in its upkeep. It is thus no wonder that this new castle was described as early as 1453 as "until now uninhabited and hence desolate and ephemeral".

The treasury completed in 1981 contains over five hundred works of exquisite craftsmanship made of gold, silver, ivory and porcelain, including this mounted knight from the late 16th century.

The ruins of Baldeneltz still look down threateningly on Burg Eltz, thus giving palpable shape to an exciting period in medieval history, especially as some of the stone missiles catapulted at Burg Eltz are now exhibited in the inner ward. It should be remembered here that castle sieges, contrary to popular opinion, were the exception rather than the rule prior to the 15th century. Yet it is this which makes those few sieges that can be reconstructed all the more important from the point of view of military history and indeed the history of castles too.

The restoration of the castle between 1845 and 1888 as also its development for the purposes of modern tourism both took a conservative approach to the late Gothic interiors and added only such furnishings as would help depict castle life as it really was in the late Middle Ages. The bed chamber with its colourful floral paintings and heavy wooden ceiling in the Rübenach House is especially impressive, as is the pretty oratory with its delightfully decorative wing doors.

The colourful bed chamber in the Rübenach House has largely retained its 15th century appearance, despite 19th century restoration work. The pretty fireplace, four-poster bed and small oriel, which also served as an oratory, are all late Gothic. The oratory

can be closed by two painted wing doors.

Münzenberg -
crown of the Wetterau

View of the twin-towered Münzenberg, which ranks among the greatest medieval castles in Germany. It began as a much more

modest building in the last third of the 12th century. The western tower (left), northern great hall and other courtyard buildings were added only after the Münzenberg lineage had died out.

High up on a basalt mountain in the Wetterau and visible for miles around, there is an impressive, twin-towered castle which dominates the surrounding countryside in a way that almost no other castle does: This is the Münzenberg - one of the most thrilling and most interesting castles produced by the German Middle Ages.

The Münzenberg is enthroned on an extensive hill-top, delimited by a round tower at each end. It thus gives the impression of having been the result of a homogeneous, harmonious concept. But appearances are deceptive.

Kuno I of Münzenberg, chamberlain to Kaiser Friedrich Barbarossa, sought to advertise his prosperity and elevated position by building a huge castle containing, among other things, an attractive great hall, a grand keep and a high, battlemented curtain wall.

The lords of Münzenberg died out in 1255, five years after their castle had been partially destroyed. The estate was shared by two brothers-in-law, who proceeded to enlarge it by the addition of a second great hall and a second keep. It was thus neither military nor defensive considerations which led to the

The southern great hall, built around 1170/80, is remarkable for its outstanding stone masonry and impressive, richly ornamented, arched windows. The opulence of the ornamentation served as a pointer to the high social status of the lords of the manor. The southern great hall is now considered a masterpiece of secular, Romanesque architecture in Germany.

The castle was built by the "ministeriales" of Münzenberg in the last third of the 12th century. The building work was both commissioned and financed by the king, who wanted more castles to protect his extensive domains in the Wetterau against attack by power-hungry nobles. At this time, the job of administering the imperial demesnes went increasingly to loyal, unfree knights or "ministeriales", which eventually resulted in their becoming a highly influential, noble class in their own right.

building of the two towers, but rather a power struggle between the two co-owners of the castle, each of whom sought to manifest his claim to power with his particular ensemble of hall and keep.

The symbolism concealed in every medieval castle is thus especially palpable here at Münzenberg.

Mespelbrunn -
the island castle deep in the Spessart forest

The energetic and strict Prince Bishop Julius Echter (1573-1617) was the most famous member of the line of Echters of Mespelbrunn. It was he, with the aid of the Jesuits, who pushed through the Counterreformation in Franconia, who reorganized the Catholic church and became co-founder of the Catholic League.

This romantic, island castle, nestling among the green, densely wooded hills of the Spessart, acquired worldwide fame thanks to an exciting film about the notorious bandits who used to wreak havoc in these dark forests. Today, this dreamy, island castle, delightfully reflected in the lake surrounding it, is a hot tip for both national and international tourists alike, even if they are unlikely to find the sinister hostel with its creaking stairs supposedly situated nearby - at least according to the film.

To art historians, the name Mespelbrunn has come to stand for a gem of Renaissance architecture, while to historians, the castle is most important as the birthplace of the famous Bishop of Würzburg, Julius Echter.

Mespelbrunn was originally built by the nobleman forester, Hans Echter, who is alleged to have accompanied his lord, the Archbishop Johann of Mainz, on a stag hunt in the year 1412. After a wild chase, the Bishop collapsed and cried out desperately for water. Echter thereupon used what little strength he himself had left to drag his lord to a spring, some distance away in a remote valley. To thank the forester for saving his life, the Bishop enfeoffed him this very valley - together with the surrounding forests - which at that time was called the "Espelborn". Over the years, the name gradually turned into today's "Mespelbrunn".

Seven years later, Hans Echter built himself a typical Franconian "Weiherhaus" or pond house, consisting of a small, residential tower built on a tiny island. As time passed, however, this tower proved not only too small but also too vulnerable. This was the 1420s, when the Hussites, a militant religious movement from Bohemia, were launching raids into Franconia. Their horseback troops were able to advance fast and penetrate deep into the Franconian countryside, looting and plundering as they went. It did not take long before their reputation alone evoked such terror that numerous castles, churches, towns and markets had to be refortified.

Hans Echter, the son of the original lord, also moved with the times. From 1427 onwards, he worked hard on the conversion of the old "Weiherhaus" into a solid, residential castle - although it was not until a century later that it was to become the beautiful Renaissance castle it is today.

Julius Echter was born on March 18, 1545, just a few years before this restyling of his ancestral home began. He soon developed an unusually strong personality and so became the Prince Bishop of Würzburg at the tender age of just 28. In this position, he was both resolute and successful in representing the interests of the Counterreformation. He also proved a great builder, however, not only commissioning churches up hill and down dale but also, in the late 16th century, founding both the Julius Hospital and the University of Würzburg. The restoration of Würzburg's Fortress Marienburg can also be attributed to him.

In 1665, the last of the Echters of Mespelbrunn died childless with the result that the castle passed to the barons of Ingelheim, who restored it in a romantic style and still own it today.

The picturesque, waterside castle was built between 1427 and 1434, when the original "Weiher-haus" was enlarged. The keep, residential buildings and corner tower all originate from this period. The castle was redesigned in the 19th century, when the archway at the entrance was added.

Heidelberg -
the Renaissance at its most sublime

Scarcely any other city profited quite so much from German Romanticism and its glorious student days as did the much-lauded city of Heidelberg. This was by no means least owing to the huge, sprawling castle ruins which dominate both the Neckar valley and the little towns strung along its banks. The castle started life as the home of the Counts Palatine and the Wittelsbach family, who in the early decades of the 16th century added some enormous artillery towers with walls several metres thick and so transformed the castle into an unassailable bulwark.

Whereas even around 1530, the Elector Ludwig V of the Palatinate was still building in the late Gothic style, the humanist-educated Elector Ottheinrich changed this when he introduced the ultra-modern Renaissance style of architecture to Germany in the mid-16th century. This new style, however, was by no means as modern or as new as its euphoric reception and rapid spread throughout Europe might lead one to believe. Having emerged in Italy in the 15th century, it was in fact a deliberate attempt to revive the architectural elements of the ancients. Affluent nobles and princes, both secular and ecclesiastical, as well as rich patricians all needed new, ever more spectacular forms of expression with which to demonstrate their high social status and it was in the beaux arts that they found both their inspiration and their materials. The seemingly chaotic asymmetry of late medieval facades was abandoned in favour of the logic and rigour of classical structures. It was this attempt to produce clearly delimited facades that marked the debut of both geometry and symmetry in the world of architecture - a process which reached its zenith in the Baroque and Classical era. To lend these somewhat plain and businesslike facades rather more glory and joie de vivre, however, they were adorned with numerous ornamental features such as sweeping gables and splendid oriels. It was this, combined with the allusions to classical architecture, that compelled the vertical thrust of late Gothic architecture (Cologne Cathedral, Strasbourg Minster) to surrender to the horizontal thrust of Classicism.

Between 1550 and 1600, Schloss Heidelberg was transformed into a truly superb example of Renaissance-style architecture. It was above all the Ottheinrich's Building, built under the Elector Ottheinrich in 1556-60 that was to overshadow all other Renaissance buildings for decades to come. Visitors were greeted by an unbelievably detailed abundance of pilasters, columns, capitols, friezes, consoles, pediments, facet-cut stonework and statues, the purpose of which was to overwhelm them and impress upon them a sense of their own smallness. The triumphal arch with its pompous coat-of-arms was crowned with a bust of the man who commissioned it, who thus far erected a monument to himself, which at the same time became the focal point of the castle.

In addition to the fantastic architecture, the castle has two more attractions for its modern-day visitors, namely Germany's largest surviving wine cask and the German Apothecary Museum. The latter was first founded in Berlin in 1937 and moved to Heidelberg twenty years later. Today, it brings the past back to life in Ottheinrich's Building.

The castle buildings, most of which date from the late Middle Ages and the Renaissance, crowd together on the hillside above Heidelberg. The splendid residential buildings are interspersed by huge artillery towers - all of them stoney witnesses to the power once enjoyed by the electors of the Palatinate, who held court here from 1329 onwards. This magnificent castle was destroyed by French troops in 1689 and again in 1693.

The Heidelberger Wine Cask commissioned by the Elector Carl Theodor in 1751 had a capacity of 220,000 litres and was built to hold the wine dues rendered by the vintners of the Palatinate. It was also an attempt to win the bizarre "Cask War", in which Germany's electors competed to see who could build the largest wine cask. The Königsteiner cask, however, was larger than that in Heidelberg (cf. Königstein).

Hohenzollern -
a glorious monument to a royal house

Times change, and with them our tastes too. There can be no better proof of this than Schloss Hohenzollern. Unlike today's visitors, most of whom are delighted by what they see, Kaiser Wilhelm II was positively disgusted when he visited the seat of the Hohenzollerns in November 1893. What he despised most of all was the neo-Gothic restyling of the Zollerns' ancestral home. Wherever he looked, all he could see was one example after another of French, late Gothic architecture - and that to excess! The man who had commissioned the renovation work, King Friedrich Wilhelm IV of Prussia, could scarcely be blamed for this eyesore as the Gothic had been considered a great and intrinsically German style of building at the time the work was done. It was not until the end of the century that the

With its numerous towers and turrets and impressive, neo-Gothic architecture, the hill-top Hohenzollern, built in 1850-67 on the site of the Zollerns' ancestral home, commands superb views of the surrounding countryside. It was commissioned by the Prussian King Friedrich Wilhelm IV as a means of demonstrating the greatness and glory of the house of Zollern. Today, it houses a treasury with the crown of the Prussian Kings and various personal effects. The castle is also used as a venue for concerts, plays and exhibitions and medieval fairs and Christmas markets are also a regular feature at the site.

St Michael's chapel, built in 1454 and restored in neo-Gothic style in the 19th century, is worth visiting for its 13th century painted glass windows and the three 11th century reliefs it houses.

Germans discovered, much to their dismay, that Gothicism had not merely been adopted by their arch-enemy, France, but actually epitomized a typically French, rather than German, style of architecture.

Of course it was too late to change anything by then. Neo-Gothicism had already found its way into countless restoration projects as well as a number of new castles, including some built by the Prussian royal family, such as Stolzenfels am Rhine (see p. 48).

The only words of praise to be extracted from the appalled Kaiser Wilhelm back in November 1893 were those reserved for the magnificent views to be had from the castle. When it

came to the restoration of his own Hohkönigsburg in Alsace in 1900, however, he was careful to demand only Romanesque structures and a Germanic architectural style.

Friedrich Wilhelm, meanwhile, was firmly convinced that he had rebuilt the seat of his blue-blooded dynasty in a style characteristic of the German nobility. He got the idea for this gigantic project during a depressing tour through the delapidated interior of the castle in his days as Crown Prince back in 1819. The first attempts to renovate the Hohenzollern had to be aborted when the castle was struck by lightning in 1844. Friedrich Wilhelm, however, had in any case been so dissatisfied with the results that he decided to engage a new architect by the name of August Stüler, a pupil of the famous Karl Friedrich Schinkel.

The splendid castle with its towers and turrets erected by Stüler between 1850 and 1867 on top of a hill visible for miles around largely eliminated the remains of its medieval predecessor. The only building to be spared was St Michael's chapel, built in 1454. In all other respects, the so-called restoration work actually entailed the erection of a completely new building, the sole purpose of which was to illustrate the past and present power of the Zollerns as impressively as possible. This worked especially well in the "Stammbaumhalle" or Hall of Genealogy, which depicts the emergence and growth of the powerful Zollern family, and in the splendid "Grafensaal", which positively radiates regal glory.

The completion of the restoration work on October 3, 1867 was celebrated as a major national event. But it wasn't long before tastes began to change and criticism of the castle - including that levelled by the Kaiser himself - caused the new Hohenzollern to be regarded as a tasteless caricature.

Now, with the hindsight of over a century, Schloss Hohenzollern can be classified as an outstanding cultural monument of considerable historical significance. Together with a number of other spectacular examples of neo-Gothic architecture, among them Neuschwanstein, Stolzenfels and Kreuzenstein near Vienna, it helped inspire an interest in and enthusiasm for the Middle Ages in the mid-19th century.

Castle fans will enjoy a tour of the six, large bastions with which Colonel Prittwitz surrounded the castle in 1847. Those for whom that is not reason enough for a visit should remember that even Kaiser Wilhelm II found the views magnificent.

The house of Zollern split into a Swabian and a Franconian line as far back as the 12th century. It was the Franconian line which was to give the name of Zollern the glory it later enjoyed. It was this line of the family which produced the influential Burgraves of Nuremberg (see p. 80), the Margraves of Brandenburg and later the Kings of Prussia and German Kaisers.

The original Zollern castle, dating back to the 11th century, went up in flames in 1423 after its owner, Friedrich der Öttinger Count of Zollern, had not only plundered the surrounding lands but had also got into a feud with the Swabian imperial cities, which ultimately defeated him. The ban on any attempts to rebuild the castle imposed upon its destruction was not lifted until 1453/54, by Kaiser Friedrich III.

The splendid castle interior was completed in 1853-1867 and successfully conveys a sense of the the Zollerns' regal glory. Besides the magnificent "Grafensaal", the Blue Salon with its sophisticated furnishings is also a great eye-catcher.

Hohenasperg -
often embattled, often seized

Over the centuries, the fortress which the Swabian League bombarded so successfully in 1519 gradually turned into a huge national fortress. Starting in 1534 , the old bailey with its small towers (visible in the background) was reinforced by the addition of bastions, earthworks and wide ditches while additional fortifications were added at the foot of the hill. By the end of the 17th century, the Hohenasperg was considered one of the most important national fortresses in Württemberg.

The soil of the little town of Asperg is steeped in history. On a small hill to the south of the town there is the "Kleinaspergle" tumulus, the richly adorned grave of a Celtic prince, just as nearby Grafenbühl can boast the only Sphinx north of the Alps.

The Hohenasperg which overlooks the town of Asperg and is supposedly the highest hill in Swabia, became the seat of a Franconian count in the early Middle Ages and was therefore mentioned in the Geographus Ravennae as the "Aszis" as early as the 5th century.

The Counts Palatine of Tübingen probably erected the first castle here some time after 1181. Four years after this castle had

After the Battle of Nördlingen during the Thirty Years' War, the fortress was besieged from August 1634 to July 1635. The fortifications were modernized towards the end of the 17th century and in the years that followed the Hohenasperg came to be used both as a garrison and as a prison. The poet, Christian Daniel Schubart, for example, was incarcerated here from 1777-1787 and spent 377 days of his confinement in a dark dungeon.

Today, the fortress contains a hospital penitentiary, which means that access to the fortress is limited. It is nevertheless well worth a visit, if only on account of the superb views.

The outer gate of the Veste Hohenasperg, also known as the "Löwentor" or "Lion's Gate". This was built in 1675 during an expansion project according to plans by Matthias Weiss. The gate acquired its name from the lion's head crowning it.

passed into the hands of the dukes of Württemberg, it was destroyed by the imperial army of Heinrich VII in the course of the Reich war of 1312. During the reconstruction work, a village was added which in 1510 was granted a town charter. Nine years later, when the Swabian League drove Duke Ulrich of Württemberg out of the region, Georg of Frundsberg had the fortress heavily and successfully bombarded - an incident which has been preserved for us in a pen-and-ink drawing by Albrecht Dürer. The severe damage suffered during this attack required comprehensive rebuilding work, although this was not commenced until 1534. As the fortress could not be expanded as long as it was surrounded by the town, however, the town was summarily uprooted and moved down into the valley without further ado.

Rothenburg -
a medieval jewel

This photo shows how Rothenburg has been able to preserve its medieval appearance, despite extensive war damage. The large, Gothic church of St Jakob towers over the walled town centre while the 16th century Old Town Hall is visible on the right.

There can be no more impressive proof of the unusual appeal and popularity among tourists the Middle Ages have acquired over the past few decades than the small, Franconian town of Rothenburg. Every year, hundreds of thousands of visitors from all over the world saunter down its narrow, cobbled streets, hoping to get a sense of life as it was lived a thousand years ago. After expecting to find a dreamy, picturesque little town, they are often amazed to discover that Rothenburg has everything modern-day tourism demands - from a Christmas market open all year round to an excellent museum of criminology and opulent medieval banquets.

For those interested in history, however, Rothenburg does not become genuinely exciting until you wander away from the crowded main streets and into the little alleys and along the city walls. And even if not everything which looks old really is old, the town does have a strange magic about it - a magic which is almost impossible to escape. This is all the more remarkable given that Rothenburg was heavily bombed just a few days before the end of the Second World War. With great care, and great far-sightedness too, the higgledy-piggledy old buildings have gradually been rebuilt, brick by brick.

The history of Rothenburg began at the end of the 10th century with the building of the "Roten Burg" or "Red Castle" on a bend in the river Tauber. The colour red comes from the red sandstone used to build not only the castle but most of the town as well. Rothenburg was granted a town charter by Kaiser Barbarossa (Friedrich I) as far back as 1172. It was not until a century or so later, however, that King Rudolf of Habsburg elevated Rothenburg to the status of "Reichstadt" or "imperial city", meaning a city directly subordinate to the king. This meant considerable economic and administrative advantages for the town. After all, the kaiser was hardly ever there and Rothenburg was therefore able to develop much more freely and independently than many other towns at that time.

Rothenburg cleverly exploited these freedoms and thanks to its astute trading and territorial policies, quickly became extremely wealthy. This prosperity and growth, however, also caused its no less acquisitive neighbours, namely the bishopric of Eichstätt and burgraves of Nuremberg, to view it with both envy and disquiet.

The most serious threat, however, came from a most unexpected quarter - namely from Kaiser Karl IV himself, who in 1349, doubtless for financial reasons, decided to pledge the town to none other than its arch-enemy, the bishopric of Würzburg. This kind of pledging turned out to be a most convenient means of refilling the state's empty coffers, especially as the imperial cities were prepared to do just about anything to free themselves from this dependency on their new masters and could therefore be pledged again and again. Rothenburg, whose excellent financial situation was thanks by no means least to its Jewish community, redeemed itself from this involuntary attachment three years later and in 1355, elicited a concession from the kaiser to the effect that it would never be pledged again. Although Rothenburg continued to flourish for several years under the agile leadership of its burgomaster, Heinrich Toppler, the next storm clouds were already gathering. This was because the princes, supported by a vacillating king, had decided to join forces in an attempt to curb the power of the cities. Whereas in 1408, Rothenburg once again succeeded in concluding what for it was an advantageous peace, the opposition it faced ultimately proved too strong. Countless feuds and the battles of the Reformation and Thiry Years' War ate away at both the wealth and importance of the city over the years.

Although the fortified city wall had been able to protect the people of Rothenburg against many an onslaught, in 1631, it was not the wall but the so-called "Master Drink" which ultimately saved them. Forces belonging to Tilly's Catholic League had besieged the town and were about to seize it and loot it for all it was worth when Burgomaster Nusch made a bet with the enemy to the effect that if he succeeded in drinking a huge tankard of wine in one gulp, the city would be spared. Thank God he succeeded!

The imperial city had a separate gate to the castle too. This 14th century gate tower is the highest tower in Rothenburg. The building in front of it with its round towers, toll house and sentry house and attractive coat-of-arms, was not added until the 16th century.

Rothenburg's first city wall was built as far back as the end of the 12th century and then expanded and modernized over the centuries to follow, when both the Röder Gate and Markus Tower were added. The city wall not only protected the inhabitants and their property but also served as proof of the town's high status and prosperity.

Nuremberg -
bone of contention between the kaiser, citizens and burgraves

The so-called Heathens' Tower can be seen here in front of the great hall and the famous, two-storey chapel. Despite its name, this tower was built during the period of the Hohenstaufen kaisers and used to serve as the keep of the old imperial castle. The burgraves' castle and imperial castle were formerly two completely separate installations.

The overriding importance of the castle and city of Nuremberg for medieval Germany is apparent from the fact that no fewer than 32 German rulers repeatedly resided here, some of them - such as Kaiser Ludwig the Bavarian - even several times a year.

Kaiser Heinrich III held court at the castle he founded as early as 1050. Over three hundred years later, in the year 1356, Kaiser Karl IV ordained that every newly elected German king should hold his first session of court in Nuremberg.

This impressive castle, which over the centuries has come to tower over the city below, was viewed by the city's inhabitants not only with pride but also with growing concern and even resentment. This was owing to the arrival in 1192 of the new burgraves of Hohenzollern, who proceeded to make themselves at home on the eastern part of the castle plateau. Their political ambitions pointed to an unusually strong craving for power as well as expansionism, meaning that it did not take long before they became embroiled in serious conflicts with the prosperous

and similarly expansionist imperial city. The city, for its part, had been blessed with the trusteeship of the imperial castle back in the 14th century and consequently had direct influence on and access to the castle plateau.

While the Hohenzollern dynasty, as the margraves of Brandenburg and Ansbach, continued to enlarge their domains outside Nuremberg, their influence within the city and the castle steadily declined. Calamity crept up on them, starting in 1362-67, when the city sealed off the burgraves' fortress by erecting a huge fortified wall. Ten years later, it took advantage of the absence of the Burgrave to erect a high lookout tower, the so-called "Luginsland", right next to his castle. The incensed Burgrave complained to the Kaiser that the city had hedged in his castle to such an extent that he was no longer lord of his own lordship. But his complaints fell on deaf ears and there was worse still to come: A decade later, the city forcibly occupied the burgraves' castle which in 1420 was finally razed to the ground during a feud with the Duke of Bavaria-Palatinate. At their wits' end and exhausted by years of continuous quarreling and repeated setbacks, the burgraves finally left Nuremberg and in 1427 sold their half of the castle to the imperial city. Nuremberg could now concentrate fully on the expansion and safeguarding of its territories and trade relations.

In the years that followed, the castle and city merged to form an impressive fortification which, above all in 1538-45, was furnished with modern bastions, outer fortifications and wide moats by the Italian fortifications expert, Antoni Fazuni Malthese.

Despite severe bombing during the Second World War, the largely restored castle has retained its best buildings, among them the famous two-storey, Romanesque chapel.

The long silhouette of the imperial castle consists of the Sinwell Tower (left) and the main castle (right half of the photo). The Heathens' Tower, which contains the chapel, is at the other end of the plateau, as is the adjoining great hall. The two-storey chapel has a large opening in the floor of the upper storey, thus connecting the ground floor and first floor. This meant the kaiser could attend church services and receive the blessing unnoticed by other worshippers. The chapel and great hall were probably built under Kaiser Friedrich I, or Barbarossa, in the late 12th century. Archaeologists have uncovered parts of the walls of the original fortress, first built in 1050, under the great hall. The burgraves' castle was originally to the left of its imperial counterpart shown on the photo.

Prunn -
keeper of the Nibelungenlied

Bold and defiant, the castle crouches on its narrow precipice, the moat surrounding it rendering it still more unassailable. The huge keep with its bulging stonework is situated right at the front of the castle to protect the buildings behind it. This keep, together with the curtain wall and the great hall, are probably among the oldest buildings in the castle, dating from around 1200. As was customary in those days, the great hall was built on the leeside of the precipice. The coat-of-arms with the rearing horse is that of the Fraunberger family, lords of Prunn from 1311-1567.

Despite the havoc wrought by the construction of the Rhine-Main-Danube Canal, this castle, situated high up above the river Altmühl on a bizarre, limestone outcrop, has lost almost nothing of its wild, romantic image and continues to attract thousands of tourists year in year out.

Yet very little is known about this castle, which is mentioned - at least indirectly - together with a certain "Wernherus de Prunne" in documents dating from as far back as 1037. As no remains of this original castle have been found, there is still some doubt as to where exactly the said Werner actually lived. In 1288, the lords of Laaber sold the castle to Duke Ludwig of Bavaria, who enfeoffed it to the Fraunbergers of Haag in 1311. This family finally purchased it in 1338 and continued to name themselves after their newly acquired seat right up until 1567. Not only that, they even embellished the wall of the castle facing the valley, and hence the most visible part of the castle, with the rearing red horse of their family coat-of-arms.

At Prunn, the Fraunbergers cultivated a sophisticated, courtly lifestyle, as is evident not only from the frescos it contains but also from a handwritten document found there shortly after 1567. This document is a handwritten copy of the famous Nibelungenlied dating from the 14th century - and hence a great literary treasure.

Hans Fraunberger (died 1428) was a celebrated and much-admired jouster in his day. After the Fraunberger lineage died out, the castle changed hands several times and each of its new owners had minor or even major work done on the castle. In 1604, for example, the gatehouse and bowers were added, followed by extensive repair work in 1631. Finally, in 1672, the castle passed to the Jesuit College of Ingolstadt, at whose instigation the chapel was likewise renovated in the year 1700. In 1827, the young King Ludwig I made the preservation of the castle a personal concern of his, although it was not until 1946 that restoration work on what was now a state-owned, national monument really got under way.

With its breathtaking location, self-contained and compact architecture and massive keep, Burg Prunn combines all the "classical" attributes of a medieval nobleman's castle: It is not just a fortress, but also a demonstration of the power, pride, unassailability and unyieldingness of its lords.

The so-called court room. As in most furnished castles, neither the furniture nor the function of this room is original. In the Middle Ages, there was no

strict allocation of specific functions to specific rooms. Most habitable rooms were used for a number of different purposes at the same time.

Landshut -
home of the "rich dukes"

The proud and mighty Burg Trausnitz had long since gallantly withstood all the assaults launched against it, had long since adjusted to the idea of a peaceful retirement as a tourist attraction when, at 4 am on October 21, 1961, calamity struck in the most curious and unexpected way. A single immersion heater triumphed where centuries earlier whole armies had failed: It reduced much of the castle to an ignominious heap of rubble.

The fire spread greedily from room to room. The prince's apartments, the "Georgrittersaal" above the chapel and royal apartments of King Ludwig II were all lost in the inferno and the so-called Italian annex with its famous "Fool's Staircase" was severly damaged.

Today, most of the laborious and cost-intensive reconstruction and restoration work is finished and Burg Trausnitz once again towers majestically over the old part of Landshut - an impressive testimony to the power once exercised by the house of Wittelsbach, the family which for centuries produced Bavaria's dukes, electors and kings.

One contemporary report claims that Duke Ludwig I of Kelheim began building both the castle and town in the year 1204. Thirty-one years later, it was visited by Kaiser Friedrich II, who found it to be an attractive building and an important centre of courtly culture, much frequented by famous minnesingers such as Walther von der Vogelweide, Neidhardt von Reuenthal, Thannhäuser and Reinbot von Durne. Despite this, however, the exact history of this castle continues to elude us. According to the latest research, the famous Wittelsbach Tower, a huge, residential tower on the city-side of the castle which dominates the entire site, was not part of the original castle, as was once thought, but rather was added in the late 15th century. Only the impressive, twin-towered castle gate, the chapel and parts of the bowers can be attributed to the year 1240, whereas the oldest visible walls inside the prince's apartments and in the Alte Dürnitz must be dated around twenty years later.

Burg Landshut enjoyed a golden age under the so-called "rich dukes" Heinrich XVI (1393-1450), Ludwig IX (1450-79) and Georg (1479-1503), all of whom did a lot of work on the castle. It was Ludwig X (1516-45), however, who made the fortress his seat of government and transformed it into an attractive Renaissance castle. From 1545 onwards, it served as the official residence of the Bavarian crown princes. These included Prince Wilhelm, who in 1568, celebrated his marriage to Renata of Lorraine in the nearby city of Munich with a pomp and splendour rarely seen in those days and after three whole weeks of feasting moved to his freshly painted castle, together with his bride and a whole army of servants, cavaliers, musicians, painters, comedians, sculptors, architects, goldsmiths, gem-cutters, decorators, dwarfs and jesters.

Of all the entertainments they were offered, the young couple liked the Commedia dell'arte best - in fact so much so that from 1575 onwards, they had the castle restyled in the Italian manner. Italian artists created exquisite wall decorations, including the imaginative tromp d'oeil, the so-called "Fool's Staircase"

View of the main castle. Until recently, the Wittelsbach Tower in the foreground was thought to be the oldest part of the castle dating from the year 1204. The latest research, however, indicates that this tower was not built until the late 15th century, even though it contains an older fragment which was integrated in the new building by several segmental arches (bottom right of the tower). The gable of the prince's apartments, once the great hall, can be seen protruding behind the tower. The castle did not acquire the appearance it has today until the era of the so-called "rich dukes" in the 15th and 16th centuries.

which, with its amusing, life-size figures, is very much reminiscent of the wit and esprit of the Commedia dell'arte. The groom's father, however, Duke Albrecht V, did not find anything amusing about the simple-mindedness with which his son set about squandoring the family fortune. After having his wings clipped, the now somewhat chastened and melancholy crown prince, his condition further exacerbated by a high fever, suddenly found himself unable to bear the noise and joviality of life at the castle and consequently fled it, with the intention of leading a more sober and spartan life elsewhere.

The interior decorations could not disguise the fact that Burg Trausnitz was still strategically important. An incredibly detailed wooden model of the castle and town built by the cabinet-maker, Jacob Sandtner of Straubing in the year 1572, confronts us with an astonishingly heavily fortified castle, whose

The early Gothic chapel contains not only much of its splendid original decor but also late Gothic paintings. The crucifixion altar by the Old Bavarian Master, dated around 1460/70, is especially important to art history. The two wings show the two St Johns.

extensive, but dangerously exposed outer castle was especially well protected by towers and curtain walls. Behind this, there were countless commercial buildings, workshops, offices and dwellings, all indicating what a large and populous household and court once resided at the castle.

The fortifications were again upgraded in the aftermath of the Thirty Years' War (1618-48). Yet the sovereign prince's interest in this castle, which naturally was very expensive to maintain, began to wane as early as the 18th century. After providing premises first for a woollens and silk factory, the castle went on to serve as an up-market prison, before being converted into a lazaretto and cholera hospital. It was not until the reign of King Ludwig I and that of Ludwig II that its inexorable decline was finally halted. The latter had splendid royal apartments built here in 1869, although he never actually used them. In 1923, the Bavarian Castles Administration took over the maintenance of the castle.

Besides the Alte Dürnitz, the "Fool's Staircase" and inside of the castle, which is now a museum, the chapel of St Georg erected in 1230/40 and redesigned in the 15th century is also worth a visit on account of its well-preserved early-Gothic figures.

An excursion to the Wittelsbachs' town house, built by Duke Ludwig X in 1536 in the centre of the town is also worthwhile. This Italian-style urban palace, almost certainly attributable to Ludwig's trip to Mantua, where he visited the famous Palazzo del Tè, is something of an anomaly, situated as it is among typical, late-Gothic patricians' houses.

The famous "Fool's Staircase" in the Italian annex is attributable to the delight the newly-wed crown prince Wilhelm and his wife Renata of Lorraine took in Italian Commedia dell'arte. It was this which induced them to have the castle redesigned in the Italian style starting in 1575.

Burghausen -
the longest castle in Germany

The ridge above what is a very old river crossing and surrounded by water on three sides was identified as an excellent site for a castle as far back as the 11th century, especially as the river was an important trade route at that time. The first castle built by the Counts of Burghausen soon passed to the ducal house of Wittelsbach. Around 1255, Duke Heinrich XIII began construction of a new castle. The attractive chapel of St Elisabeth dates from this period. Burghausen acquired the shape it still has today, with its six inner wards extending for over one kilometre, under the "rich dukes" of the 15th century, most of the building work having been commissioned by Duke Georg the Rich from 1480 onwards.

The view visitors encounter from the east bank of the river Salzach is still breathtaking: Towering above the densely crowded and colourful little houses lined up along the opposite bank can be seen a seemingly endless chain of castle towers, buildings and walls. The famous author, Adalbert Stifter, once fittingly described the castle and town as having been "cut out of some old German painting and put here."

There is no shortage of superlatives, but none strong enough to convey the power and intensity inherent in this historical ensemble.

It was only under the "rich dukes" of the 15th century that Burghausen became the second most important residence after Landshut. In military terms, it was actually superior to Landshut as it was here that the "rich dukes" kept their riches, consisting of 500,000 gold ducats, pictures made of precious metals and gold bars. It was not until the Landshut War of Succession that these treasures were transported on seventy six-horse waggons to the still more secure fortress at Neuburg on the Danube. The "rich dukes", however, found the remote Burghausen to be a good place for locking up more than just their material wealth. Their wives and widows were kept here too. Many a

promising marriage ended here in misery and disgrace - at least for the duchesses, among them the Duchess of Hedwig, who in 1475 married Duke Georg the Rich in a ceremony in Landshut of incredible pomp and splendour.

It was thanks to her husband, however, that life in Burghausen had since become not just tolerable but comfortable too. In

craftsmen from throughout Bavaria were to be found working on the site at any given time.

There was, of course, a reason for this decision to transform the castle into a giant fortress: Fear of the Turks was widespread at this time. In 1453, Constantinople had fallen to the Turks in a sea of blood, despite having been considered unassailable. And

Castles often had powers of jurisdiction, which in most cases took the form of manorial courts without the power to impose the death penalty. The lucrative high courts which did indeed have the power to judge serious crimes were often reserved for the sovereign prince, and hence the lords of Burghausen. The enlargement of prisons and installation of torture chambers in castles, however, including in Burghausen, often had more to do with the 16th century Inquisition or 19th century revisionism than with medieval crime sta-

tistics. This woodcut from the year 1508 shows various methods of capital punishment all common at that time, including burning at the stake, breaking on the wheel, disembowelling, hanging and beheading, as well as "lesser" blood punishments such as the gouging out of the eyes and chopping off of the hands.

the 1480s, Duke Georg the Rich invested a fortune to the tune of 100,000 gulden in the expansion and modernization of the castle. While the interiors were furnished in great splendour and all the fittings and conveniences required for his wife's enormous household installed, the outside of the castle was converted to accommodate artillery. The six consecutive inner wards were reinforced and fosses, pompous gatehouses and turrets added wherever necessary. The town below became an integral part of the fortress and so acquired a powerful battery tower.

Incredible amounts of money and labour went into the building work required for this project between 1486 and 1488, and up to four thousand builders, masons, labourers and other

now the "infidels" were planning to take their holy war to the rest of the world as well. As far as the Moslems were concerned, the similarly "infidel" occident right there on their doorstep was both a provocation and a temptation at the same time, especially as the atrocities with which the Crusaders had ravaged the Holy Land were still fresh in the memory.

Advancing over land, the Turks had already made good progress when, in 1480, their huge fleet turned up at Rhodes - the last Christian bastion - with the intention of clearing the way to Europe by sea. Having advanced that far, nothing would have been able to stop the fanatical armies invading southeastern Europe. By an extraordinary stroke of luck, however, a mighty storm smashed the Turkish fleet just in time and so prevented the defeat of Rhodes - at least for a while. Nevertheless, the threat remained and everyone knew that the Turks would use this interruption of their advance to muster new forces for a second onslaught. The danger increased with every uneventful year that passed and as the occident was once again at odds with itself, it could do little more than sit by and watch. The fortifications on Rhodes were reinforced but no attempt was made to launch a collective offensive. The Turkish army was

marched on as far as the Austrian part of the Danube. The unsuccessful siege of Vienna in 1529 gave Central Europe a few years of respite, although it was not until 1565, when the Turkish fleet was stopped at Malta and six years later was routed by the Venetians and Spaniards near Lepanto, that the threat was banished for good.

Had the Turks advanced up the Danube, Burghausen, as the eastern-most point of the Duchy, would indeed have been put

The foremost of the inner wards has a small well-house with a deep draw well. The clock-tower dating from the 16th and 17th century was built onto the well-house.

therefore able to grow unabated, acquiring new soldiers, new weapons and new ships with every day that passed.

And as if that were not enough, the rumours and printed pamphlets detailing the cruelty and brutality of the Turks long before they actually arrived - even going so far as to claim that they ate little children - had a paralysing impact on all those who heard them. Originally intended to galvanize the population into action, this propaganda actually had the opposite effect, creating a situation of every man for himself.

This fear of the Turks remained throughout the 16th century, especially after Rhodes finally fell in 1522. Four years later, Hungary was defeated in the Battle of Mohács and the Turks

to the test. It is thus no wonder that by 1533, its walls boasted no fewer than 134 heavy cannons and bombards with a further 185 cannons and mortars housed in the armory. Thank God Burghausen never had to make use of these defences - unlike the other castles further down the river! The castle retained its strategic significance, as is apparent from the fact that its defences were modernized on a number of occasions over the centuries.

Eisenberg and Hohenfreyberg -
two castles, one hill

Among the most eye-catching sights in the Pfrontener Land are the ruins of two castles situated atop the twin peaks of a high mountain, visible from far and wide and hence one of the most spectacular castle landscapes in Europe.

The Eisenberg is the older of the two castles and was built around 1315 by the prominent Hohenegger family, which needed a new territorial base from which to pursue its quarrel with the County of Tyrol.

To demonstrate its unbroken power, the nobles of Hohenegg erected a proud, hill-top castle, consisting primarily of an extremely high curtain wall. It was Tyrol, of all places, which eventually purchased this fortress in the late 14th century and went on to enfeoff it to the Freyberger dynasty.

Eisenberg castle was built in the early 14th century. By the time it was destroyed in 1646, it had become a powerful, residential castle.

The idea of the neighbouring castle of Hohenfreyberg was born in the spring of 1418, when the eldest son of the Freybergers of Eisenberg decided not to inherit his father's castle but instead to have a lordship and castle of his own. He therefore requested the advance payment of his share of his father's estate and used it to install the tiny new lordship of Hohenfreyberg, at the centre of which was a brand-new castle. Hohenfreyberg was thus one of the last great castle-building projects of the German Middle Ages.

The age of chivalry, however, was already in both political and economic decline, its military demise having begun with the emergence of the cross-bow in the High Middle Ages and ended with the introduction of pikes and then fire arms in the Late Middle Ages (cf. Introduction).

Those feudal lords who lived off small estates with only local trading structures soon became so impoverished that they either abandoned their remote castles altogether or sought to save themselves by joining the ranks of the infamous robber barons. The age of cities and principalities, of guilds and long-distance trade, of versatile paid armies and powerful fortresses was dawning.

Not that the nobles gave up without a fight: In a last ditch attempt to avert the fate awaiting them, they began to put on elaborate displays of a chivalric splendour which in reality no longer existed. As this necessitated the revival of chivalry's traditional attributes, old suits of armour were taken out of storage, polished and patched up and, just like in the good old days, spectacular tournaments held all over the country.

This is an interesting phenomenon. Ever since the 12th century, German knights had been accustomed to putting both their horsemanship and their courage and skill with weapons to the test at public tournaments. It was here that a noble could best advertise his courtly splendour, just as it was here that he could best demonstrate his social, economic and military prowess. Thousands of visitors attended these great tournaments and because they were often surrounded by a sea of tents and stalls, they were almost never held at the castles themselves but rather on the nearby common, where the necessary infrastructure was already in place.

It was here that a knight could become rich and famous and could court the damsel of his dreams. But it was also here that he could lose not only his armour but even his life. After all, ever since jousting was introduced in the 13th century, fatal accidents had become almost commonplace. Attempts were made to reduce the risk of injury by capping the lances with blunt heads. Games of skill or strength, including stone-throwing, races, sack-races and wrestling were also introduced at this time, leading to what, by the 17th century, had come to be called "carousels". Although expensive tournaments had already been on their way out as early as the 14th century, they enjoyed a respite as a result of the revival of noble privileges in the 15th and 16th centuries. This was also the age when the nobility began doing up their castles and forming alliances, all in the vain hope that this would spare them an inglorious demise.

Friedrich of Freyberg of Hohenfreyberg went even further than this when, in 1418-32, he deliberately copied a hill-top castle dating from the 13th century - the golden age of chivalry. With its high walls and high towers, his castle was intended to prove that he was in no way inferior to his glorious forebears, that he, too, was still in possession of both wealth and power. After all, the building of a castle on such a large, hill-top site was of course much more expensive than that of a modest castle down in the valley bottom.

Indeed, this crenellated anachronism ruined not only the man who built it but also the entire family, which soon afterwards was obliged to sell the Hohenfreyberg to Austria-Tyrol.

South-eastern view of the Eisenberg (in the foreground) and Hohenfreyberg (in the background). Both castles tower above the village of Zell and castle-lake (in the distance) near Pfronten. Whereas the Eisenberg was built around 1315, the Hohenfreyberg did not appear until one hundred years later, between 1418 and 1432. It was thus the last new castle to be built during the Middle Ages and was later turned into a fortress by the Tyrolean government around 1500. Since 1995, it has been the subject of an exemplary restoration project of Europe-wide significance under the patronage of Prince Saddrudin Aga Khan. The ruins of the Eisenberg were secured back in the 1980s, thanks to the hard work and dedication of local castle enthusiasts.

Neuschwanstein -
castle of the Knight of the Swan

"We, Ludwig II, by the grace of God, King of Bavaria etc., do hereby declare that we have decided to build a new castle for us and for our court on the site where the battlements of the castles of Vorder- and Hinterhohenschwangau once towered." These are the words of the founding deed placed in the marble foundation stone of Schloss Neuschwanstein on September 5, 1869.

For Ludwig II, it marked the fulfilment of a life-long dream. Even as a child, he had often gazed up from his parents' Schloss Schwanstein (later renamed Hohenschwangau) to the dramatic ruins of the castles which had once stood on the very hill where his fairytale castle was later to be built. In his mind's eye, he doubtless saw the desolate and mysterious ruins not as they were then, but in all their former glory. He filled their rugged walls with new life. Ludwig, it should be remembered here, had a weakness for the romanticism of the chivalric age, especially for the legends of the Holy Grail and King Arthur. He also admired Richard Wagner for his revival of this period in his operas "Tristan and Isolde", "Tannhäuser", "Parsifal" and "Lohengrin". He was especially fascinated by the figure of Lohengrin, the Knight of the Swan, whose coat-of-arms, by a fortuitous coincidence, was also found in the ruins of Schwangau castle, the seat of the lords of Schwangau.

On May 13, 1868, Ludwig wrote of his intention to rebuild these ruins "in the style of an authentic medieval German castle". Yet what was declared in the plans as the "restoration of a ruined castle" in reality meant the complete removal of the same. The ruins were not only in the way but were also completely at odds with King Ludwig's romantic vision of a dreamy, cloud-capped castle. In other words: The original was not "authentic" enough and had to be replaced by a completely new castle which would be "more authentic".

From 1868 onwards, on the site of an ugly and gloomy ruined castle, Ludwig II erected a dream castle as he imagined medieval castles to have looked. It was still unfinished when Ludwig died under mysterious circumstances in the Starnberger See on June 13, 1886. Even today, parts of the castle are still awaiting completion.

This fact alone is an impressive illustration of just how far the 19th century had become removed from the true nature of the Middle Ages.

Ludwig did indeed have some very precise ideas of how his dream castle was to look: It was to consist of the great hall of the restored Wartburg, of parts of the restored Schloss Pierrefonds in France and elements of Byzantine architecture. The style prescribed by Ludwig was Romanesque - the epoch in which his chivalric idols had lived. But where would he find an architect capable of combining all these elements in a single building in such a way as to meet with the King's approval? Significantly enough, it was Christian Jank, Wagner's set-painter in Bayreuth, who submitted the plans which were eventually used. Yet even Jank's highly complex and ornate "castle in the air" proved feasible only after certain major compromises had been made.

What is interesting is that this same King who was reputed to be an introverted, inveterate day-dreamer with no sense of reality had no qualms at all about availing himself of state-of-the-art technology. Parts of the castle were built on an iron frame, for example, and inside the castle there are glass doors,

The twenty-year-old King Ludwig II in his general's uniform. This painting, dating from 1865, depicts him as a dreamy and sophisticated but also willful young monarch.

hydraulics for lowering and raising the dining table, mechanical winches for the huge chandeliers, hot and cold running water for the kitchen, fully automatic spits and a central intercom system with which to summon servants.

Tastefully worked furnishings, colourful frescos and delicate mosaics are to be found throughout the costly and highly detailed interiors, of which the so-called Minstrels' Hall and Throne Room are but the most splendid examples.

Linderhof-
King Ludwig's miniature castle

The smallest of all the royal castles was inspired by the impressions King Ludwig II of Bavaria acquired on a visit to the World Exhibition in Paris in 1867. While in Paris, he decided to view the famous royal Palace of Versailles, built for Louis XIV (from 1678), also known as the "Sun King", who made history with his pregnant declaration "l'Etat c'est moi" or "the state - that's me." He was one of the most powerful and greatest absolutist rulers and maintained a huge royal household. The more his squandering increased and craving for still more splendour grew, the more his people starved and suffered. The French Revolution of 1789, which eventually stripped the French nobil-

ity of its powers, was soon to be heard knocking angrily on the great doors of Versailles.

Ludwig II, meanwhile, obviously not only envied his namesake, but was also full of uncritical admiration for him, which is why he tried to imitate him - as far as was possible for a monarch who was not only relatively unimportant but had also been deprived by the Prussian royal family of what little political powers he had once had. Ludwig II was indeed a bored and unhappy king who, having virtually nothing to do, increasingly sought refuge in his own dreamworld. An equestrian statue of his idol, King Louis XIV, in the vestibule of the

The delightful miniature castle was built in 1870-76 and was the only castle King Ludwig II inhabited for any length of time. Ludwig himself attended to numerous details during the planning and building of the castle and, much to the chagrin of the architect, builders and craftsmen, was forever fussing about some minor aspect of their work. The statue of Venus in the round temple, for example, had to be given a new hairdo, because Ludwig thought her tied-back hair made her look too much like a cook. The splendour of the Rococco-style interiors is especially apparent in the mirror-lined hall, the audience room and bedroom.

It was a motif from the Tannhäuser saga which gave Ludwig the idea of building this artificial Venus Grotto, which in reality is an ultramodern structure. Lined with artificial cliffs, stalactites and stalagmites, this romantic cave contains an iron frame, an underwater wave generator, a warm-water heating system, electrodynamic generators and a rainbow projector.

new Schloss Linderhof is proof of his weakness for the Sun King.

Ludwig II erected his own Versailles somewhat later at Herrenchiemsee. The pastoral, Rococco Schloss Linderhof, on the other hand, adopted only certain, carefully selected elements of the French model and was intended primarily as a cosy refuge for a king who loathed urban life.

In 1870, Ludwig commissioned an architect with the planning of the Linderhof in one of his favourite childhood haunts - the remote Graswang valley, not far from the Ettal Monastery, where his father had once had a hunting lodge built.

Despite its appealing appearance and extravagant furnishings, Ludwig's new castle differed in one important respect from all other royal castles: It was small. Everything in the castle was deliberately kept small - everything except the fountains, that is, which were actually higher than those at Versailles. The purpose of these huge fountains was to make the tiny castle appear not so much tinier as further away. In this way, the park and castle acquired a spatial depth which in reality they lacked.

Ludwig livened up his miniature castle with a short cascade with a Monopteros Temple, a hermitage and, above all, a large, artificial grotto, based on a motif from the Tannhäuser saga (cf. Neuschwanstein).

Schloss Nymphenburg-
the Wittelsbachs' summer residence

The pompous palace visible today is the result of the early 18th century expansion of the original, Italian-

style villa built in 1664-76. The original villa still exists inside the central tract of the palace.

When his son and next-in-line, Max Emanuel, was born in the year 1662, the Elector Ferdinand Maria gave his wife, Adelaide of Savoy, an estate to the west of the city of Munich. Shortly afterwards, his vivacious and intelligent young wife used the site to build a summer villa in Italian Baroque style, complete with pleasure garden. The only ornamentation on what was otherwise a simple, plain building were the outside staircases leading up to it from the courtyard and the garden.

In the early 18th century, the Elector Max Emanuel enlarged this modest seat to create a spacious, strictly symmetrical palace in the middle of a vast park. French, Italian and German artists and craftsmen from all the most important cultural centres in Europe were hired for this task. The architects were Zuccalli of Graubünden, the gardener's son, Joseph Effner, of Dachau and

merous lines of view, canals and ponds and extensive ornamental shrubberies.

The Baroque park also features three miniature castles. Max Emanuel commissioned Joseph Effner with the construction of two of these, namely a pagoda and a "Badenburg", or bathing house, next to the main canal. The pagoda was to be a - tea-house, containing a Chinese salon, a cabinet, lacquerwork paintings and Chinese wallpaper made of rice straw. This was very much in keeping with the fashion for all things Chinese raging through Europe at that time. The "Badenburg" was a habitable bathing house with an unusually large and - unique in 18th century Europe - heated pool.

The "Magdaleneklause", the third of these miniature castles, was built by Johann Effner in the style of a mock ruin to which

The central tract of the palace was redesigned by the Electors Max III Joseph and Max IV Joseph. Under King Ludwig I of Bavaria (1825-48), the old dining hall was converted into a "Gallery of Beauty" in which portraits of the most beautiful women of the age were displayed.

Francois Cuvilliés of the Walloon. The result of their collective efforts, the palace which used to serve as the Wittelsbachs' summer residence, has remained virtually unchanged to this day.

The Elector's first task was to have the villa reglazed. He then added galleries and pavilions on either side, thus making the original villa the central tract of a magnificent palace with wings on each side, stables and an orangery. Some of the rooms were furnished in contemporary French style, although the jewel in the crown was the sunlight-bathed, highly colourful "Steinerne Saal", which the Elector Max III Joseph later clad in a splendid Rococco guise.

In 1702, the small pleasure garden was expanded to create a park covering a total area of approx. 200 hectares with nu-

the Electors could retreat to find relief from their affairs of state. The interior, with its grotto-like chapel and spartan furnishings is reminiscent of a hermitage.

A fourth miniature castle, the Amalienburg, has since been added to the Nymphenburger Park. In 1734-1739, the Elector Carl Albrecht had a pleasure castle built for his wife, Maria Amalia. This dainty, single-storey building, which also served as a hunting lodge, was designed by Francois Cuvilliés the Elder and is often cited as the most beautiful Rococco castle in Germany. The round, richly decorated, blue-walled hall of mirrors beneath the central dome is particularly charming.

Schloss Weissenstein -
product of a devilish mania for building

View of the grand stairwell inside the central tract which is now considered one of the greatest creations of Baroque interior design. Prince Bishop Lothar Franz von Schönborn himself helped design it. The painted ceiling is the work of Johann Rudolf Byss and shows Phoebus Apollo shedding light over all four continents.

Many princes of the 17th and 18th centuries were afflicted by a mania for building which they themselves called the "Bauwurmb", or "building worm". Lothar Franz von Schönborn (1655-1729), Prince Bishop of Bamberg, Elector and Archbishop of Mainz, Archchancellor of the Reich and builder of Schloss Weissenstein in Pommersfelden, even went so far as to describe himself as possessed by a "Teufelsbauwurmb", or devilish mania for building, which had made him addicted to this particular pursuit. His passion for building, however, served a greater purpose than mere self-aggrandizement. It also illustrated his profound knowledge and understanding of the latest architectural styles and fashions. Like many other princes, therefore, Franz Lothar became actively involved in the planning of

his edifices and in Schloss Weissenstein, created a masterpiece of Franconian Baroque.

At that time, skilful political manoeuvring on the part of the Counts of Schönborn had enabled them to obtain numerous positions of both secular and ecclesiastical power. The prince bishops of Bamberg, Würzburg, Speyer and Worms and the elector-archbishops of Mainz and Trier and the Reich vice-chancellor in Vienna were all counts of Schönborn - to name but a few.

Lothar Franz was one of the most outstanding personalities in this lineage. Thanks to a generous grant from the kaiser, he availed himself of the necessary funds to be able to erect a private palace in the monumental style near his episcopal residence in Bamberg. This private palace was to serve as a rural summer seat and hunting lodge.

Built relatively swiftly between 1711 and 1718, Schloss Weissenstein is shaped like a horseshoe, its two wings connected by two, slightly raised corner pavilions.

In architectural terms, the highlight of the palace is, of course, the central building, whose pediment features the Schönborns' coat-of-arms and is crowned by a statue of Mercury, the god of trade - which casts an interesting light on the piety of the bishop who had it built! The interior of the building consists of a spectacular and intelligently designed stairwell with double staircases, the sheer ingenuity of which has caused it to be regarded as one of the greatest creations of German Baroque architecture. The Prince Bishop himself described it as his own personal "masterpiece".

Besides the central tract, the rest of the palace also contains a number of well preserved function rooms and apartments - among them the large marble room with its monumental columns on the main floor and the oval grotto which opens out onto the garden on the ground floor.

The tripartite main building is dominated by the ornate central building. The two-storey pairs of columns and pilasters help distinguish it from the rest of the palace, thus underscoring its central importance.

Salzburg-
gigantic castle made up of seven mini-castles

This aerial photograph shows how the triangular castle can be broken down into seven smaller castles. Despite extensive conversion work from the 16th century onwards, the late Romanesque and early Gothic architecture has been well preserved. The crooked front wall of the castle with its four towers is visible on the right, the high gate tower in the centre being especially prominent. The inner ward also contains the castle church, which was rebuilt in 1841. The steward's residence, which is still intact and is visible here on the far left, is now home to the barons of Guttenberg.

Situated on a spur above the old town of Bad Neustadt an der Saale, the Salzburg has lost nothing of its immensity and majesty, despite being hedged in by the ugly box-type buildings of the Rhön Klinik.

Whereas the plethora of towers, buildings and walls appears confusing at first glance, the sheer spaciousness of this castle is truly astonishing. No fewer than nine towers and buildings, not counting the church, are still to be found scattered over the triangular site, covering an area of nearly 11,000 m2 and encircled by a 410-metre-long curtain wall. Yet as soon as you take a closer look at the layout of the castle, the confusion disappears and the method in the madness becomes clear for all to see.

There can be no doubt that the Salzburg is an extraordinary castle and one with which virtually all renowned castle researchers have concerned themselves at one time or another, arriving at the most diverse conclusions. Some traced the Salzburg's origins back to prehistoric times, while others placed it in the Early Middle Ages. Some believed it was once a royal palace visited by Charlemagne as early as 790, while others still identified it as the castle which King Otto III gave to the Bishopric of Würzburg in the year 1000. Some took the view it was built by the Salian kings in the 11th century. Yet none of these theories is correct.

appointed to reside at the Salzburg and perform various administrative tasks on behalf of the lord of the manor, namely the Bishop of Würzburg. The Salzburg thus served as an administrative centre for the episcopal domains surrounding it. And even if the walls of the Salzburg were built on top of a prehistoric defensive enclosure, there can be no doubt that the Bishop of Würzburg intended it to be a huge "Ganerbenburg", or multi-family castle, right from the start. In this respect, it differs significantly from other such castle complexes like Burg Eltz, which grew in size only very slowly. Indeed, the opposite is true of the Salzburg: Instead of expanding, the castle grew inwards. Each of the smaller castles it contains had its own keep and its own residential tower or great hall as well as the necessary utility buildings. The highest, most important and most beautiful tower, however - the gate tower with its splendidly ornate portal - belonged to the lord of the manor, namely to the bishop himself, who used it to demonstrate his power to those both inside and outside the castle.

It goes without saying that life at the castle, with so many different families and their respective retinues having to cohabit in such confined quarters, was not always peaceful, especially as there were certain things which had to be shared and collectively maintained, among them the road, the church and the well. So-called "Castle Peace Treaties" were drawn up to keep

This very interesting engraving from the year 1722 shows the Salzburg as seen from the north-west. Although the castle appears twisted and much too high, several of the buildings which were demolished shortly afterwards can nevertheless be clearly recognized.

The "Pfalz Salz" or "Salz Palace" built in the Early Middle Ages was probably located on the Veitsberg, three kilometres away, where archaeological excavations have uncovered Carolingian ruins. Our Salzburg, on the other hand, was not built until the late 12th century. Furthermore, as the curtain wall encompassing it is one of the oldest structures on the site, we know that the original castle was the same size as the castle that stands there today. There used to be a small gatehouse just behind the middle of the crooked front wall of the castle, while both front ends housed rather posh residential quarters for the steward and the advocate. Over the next few decades, various buildings were added, including the front towers and the large gate tower and five small castles, meaning that by the mid-13th century, the inner ward had to be shared by seven small castles and the castle church. At the same time, several liegemen belonging to seven noble families in the surrounding area were

the peace by preventing undesirable families from buying or inheriting a share in the castle. One such treaty dating from the year 1434 has been preserved at the castle. According to this document, the men at the castle had a rota requiring each of them to spend ten weeks working as castle warden. It was up to him to look after the keys and to open the castle gate every morning and close it every evening. His other tasks included the management of the castle, the performance of any repair work necessary and the bookkeeping.

The number of paid knights each liegeman could keep in times of peace and times of war, as well as the weapons, flour and corn he had to provide were also laid down in these treaties. Yet because this excessively large castle was never easy to defend, from the 16th century onwards it went irrevocably into decline.

Veste Coburg –
"a good egg"

The Veste Coburg has often been called the "Crown of Franconia" - and not without reason. The majestic fortress with its towers and turrets situated on top of a huge, Dolomite cliff, is indeed reminiscent of a jagged crown.

Two famous names are inextricably linked with this castle: Martin Luther and Lucas Cranach the Elder.

Martin Luther, the famous Reformer whom we will encounter again in the guise of Junker Jörg when we visit the Wartburg, stayed here at the Veste Coburg from April 23 to October 5, 1530 as a guest of the Elector of Saxony, Johann the Steadfast. It was here that he waited impatiently for his invitation to the Reichstag or imperial diet in Augsburg, where he intended to present his famous theses. Unfortunately, the obtuse members of the imperial diet decided they could dispense with Luther and so went on to ratify the Confession of Augsburg without him, this document being the basis of the Protestant faith even today. Luther, meanwhile, had not been idle either but instead had devoted his hours, days, weeks and months of fruitless waiting in the castle to his literary pursuits.

Among Martin Luther's contemporaries was Lucas Cranach the Elder of the nearby town of Kronach who, together with Albrecht Dürer, was considered one of the greatest artists of his time. In 1505, The Elector Friedrich the Wise appointed Cranach his court painter. Cranach thanked him for this appointment a year later by including a detailed painting of the Veste Coburg in his woodcut of the "Martyrdom of St Erasmus", which is now the oldest and best preserved depiction of the castle still in existence. It was also Lucas Cranach who left us with the portrait of Martin Luther, alias "Junker Jörg" (cf. Wartburg). When Cranach's patron commissioned him with the design of a new coat-of-arms, he told Cranach to be sure to paint the hen well, because it had laid the house of Saxony a good egg. The hen in this story is a reference to the Counts of Henneberg who bequeathed the "mons Coburg" to the house of Wettin in the year 1353. This legacy turned out to be a good egg, which brought the Electors of Saxony considerable good fortune.

The Veste can look back on a long history, especially as the plateau on which it was built was inhabited even in prehistoric times. By 1225, the monastery built there in the 11th century had been replaced by the first stone castle. In the course of the centuries to follow, the Counts of Henneberg and their successors, the Margraves of Meissen and Electors of Saxony, did a lot of work on the castle, which in the 17th century became a mighty fortress. Nevertheless, it soon went into decline, being used as a prison, a hospital and even an asylum.

What is remarkable is what happened to the Veste in 1838: Inspired and fascinated by the castle restorations under way on the Rhine, Duke Ernst I commissioned the famous architect, Karl Alexander von Heideloff, to renovate the Veste Coburg in neo-Gothic style, in keeping with the times. The towers were topped up and the walls decorated with countless battlements and corbelled turrets with the result that the entire edifice acquired a highly ornate silhouette.

The "Crown of Franconia" viewed from the west. The main castle towers up proudly above the outer bailey. This part of the castle was built around 1500, although some of the walls are even older. The structures remaining from the first phase of building in the early 13th century include the so-called "Blue Tower" (left), which originally served as a gatehouse. In 1906-24, the castle was restored in the Romanesque style and a number of new structures added, among them the Carl Eduard building, the roof of which is visible here in the centre of the photo.

The famous painter, Lucas Cranach the Elder, worked a lot at the castle and as court painter, was responsible for the frescos inside. This picture of Lucretia was painted in 1518.

By the end of the 19th century, however, the fickle zeitgeist had once again changed: Gothicism, which had since been exposed as a French style of architecture, was now despised, and the rediscovered, "quintessentially German", Romanesque style all the more in demand. Duke Carl Eduard of Saxony therefore commissioned the famous architect, Bodo Ebhardt (cf. Marksburg) with the restoration of the Veste Coburg to its original condition. Paradoxically, Ebhardt spent the years 1906-1924 turning what had been a pretty, hill-top castle into a colossal fortress. This is how it appears to today's visitors, despite the damage suffered during the Second World War. The works of art and outstanding collection of coaches and armory it now houses are well worth a visit.

Wartburg –
where Luther met –
and missed – the devil

Over nine centuries of German history are concentrated in the walls of the Wartburg, first founded in 1067. In 1157/58-62, the Landgrave Ludwig II built the first three storeys of the splendid great hall, which in 1190 was enlarged and in 1206/07 provided the venue for the famous "Sängerkrieg".

Today, the Wartburg ranks among the most famous of Germany's national monuments. Not only was it here, in 1206/07, that the famous "Sängerkrieg" allegedly took place, but the castle was also home to St Elisabeth, just as it was here that Luther translated the Bible and here that in 1817, five hundred members of a Protestant students' society gathered for a meeting of Germany's first grassroots, democratic opposition movement.

Perhaps things would have turned out quite differently had not Johann Wolfgang von Goethe paid the desolate castle a visit in 1777. It was his enthusiasm and his efforts to promote an awareness of the Wartburg among his contemporaries which in 1838 eventually induced the Archduke Carl Alexander of Saxony-Weimar-Eisenach to have the Wartburg restored.

According to German legend, the history of the Wartburg dates back to 1067, when Count Ludwig the Knight erected the first castle on a prominent hill-top. He used to rest here during the hunt and on one such occasion is alleged to have called out "Wart' Berg, du sollst mir eine Burg werden", meaning "Wait, mountain. You are going to become my castle!" - which is how the Wartburg derived its name.

The shrewd economic, matrimonial and territorial policies of Ludwig's descendents, the Ludowingers who in 1130 were promoted to landgraves, enabled them to acquire considerable power in Thuringia and later in Hesse too (cf. Marburg). Of all their seats, the two Thuringian castles, the Wartburg and Burg Weissensee, were the most important.

According to the latest reliable findings, the Landgrave Ludwig II began building today's castle in 1157/58, when he completed the first three storeys of the great hall. After 1190, the Landgrave Hermann I, a patron of the courtly epic famed for his generosity, enlarged the existing structure in order to be able to accommodate more guests. These included such renowned poets and singers as Walther von der Vogelweide and Wolfram von Eschenbach, who composed part of his "Parsifal" while at the Thuringian court in 1203 and 1204. It was also the Landgrave Hermann I who is reputed to have held the famous "Sängerkrieg", or singing competition, at the Wartburg in the years 1206/1207.

Hermann's son, Ludwig IV, married Elisabeth, daughter of the Hungarian king, who came to the Wartburg at the tender age of four in the year 1211 and died there twenty years later. She thus survived her husband by just four years and in 1235 was beatified on account of her extraordinary charity. She founded numerous hospitals and dedicated her life to the care of the poor and the sick. The Elisabeth Bowers, furnished in 1902-06, are a reminder of her presence at the castle.

Hereafter, despite extensive building work, the Wartburg went into decline, even though in 1521-22, it was once again to provide shelter for an important personality. After publishing his 95 theses in Wittenberg and attempting to initiate a refor-

original into German vernacular. He lived in a poorly furnished, panelled room at the Wartburg right up until March 1, 1522, when he left the castle to help control the riots then raging in Wittenberg. It was here at the Wartburg, or so legend has it, that he encountered the devil himself and hurled a bottle of ink at him in an attempt to drive him away. Efforts to retouch the ink stain cited as "proof" of this incident were observed by Goethe with great amusement in 1777.

From 1846 onwards, the rebuilding of the Wartburg was also monitored closely by Hugo von Ritgen, a young professor of architecture from Giessen. Whereas other architects wanted to transform the castle into a pompous, neo-Gothic

Medal bearing a portrait of Martin Luther. These were made upon his death in 1546.

Medal bearing a portrait of Philipp Melanchthon, the most important of the Reformers after Luther.

View of Luther's room. It was here, in 1521/22, that Luther translated the New Testament into German. It was also in this room that Luther allegedly sought to banish the devil by throwing an inkwell at him.

mation of the church, Martin Luther, a young Augustinian monk and theologian, was not only excommunicated but also outlawed by the German Reich. To his great good fortune, a number of princes sympathized with his cause, among them Friedrich the Wise of Saxony who, on May 4, 1521, had Luther summarily kidnapped and taken to the Wartburg for his own safety. Here, after growing a full head of hair and a beard and disguising himself as "Junker Jörg", he was able to devote himself to his translation of the New Testament from the Greek

dream castle, von Ritgen suggested a more conservative reconstruction of the Romanesque sections of the castle coupled with the raising of its silhouette and the addition of various picturesque details such as turrets and merlons.

Inside the great hall, the Elisabeth Gallery, Landgraves' Room and minstrel hall were decorated with fresco cycles by Moritz von Schwind. The "Festsaal" was splendidly redesigned by Michael Welter in 1867 while it was not until 1902-06 that the Elisabeth Bowers were ornamented with glass mosaics.

The great hall, of course, could have done very well without this splendour, especially as it is considered to be the best preserved example of secular Romanesque architecture north of the Alps. The ornamentation is excellent, the wonderful capitols in particular pointing to a very high standard of craftsmanship. The "Rittersaal", dining hall and chapel have an extraordinarily authentic Romanesque feel to them.

The extensive art collection with over 8,000 exhibits ranging from the 12th to 19th centuries and including a collection of beautiful textiles is also well worth a visit.

View of the Elisabeth Bowers, decorated with a glass mosaic made up of over a million fragments of coloured glass in 1902-06, by order of Kaiser Wilhelm II himself. It was here that St Elisabeth is supposed to have lived until her death in 1228.

**Names and addresses
of the castles and palaces
described:**